Masters of Mankind

Masters of Mankind

ESSAYS AND LECTURES, 1969–2013

NOAM CHOMSKY

Haymarket Books
Chicago, Illinois

Haymarket Books
PO Box 180165
Chicago, IL 60618
773-583-7884
info@haymarketbooks.org
www.haymarketbooks.org

ISBN: 978-1-60846-363-3

Trade distribution:
In the US through Consortium Book Sales and Distribution,
www.cbsd.com
In Canada, Publishers Group Canada, www.pgcbooks.ca
In the UK, Turnaround Publisher Services, www.turnaround-uk.com
All other countries, Publishers Group Worldwide, www.pgw.com

Special discounts are available for bulk purchases by organizations and
institutions. Please contact Haymarket Books for more information at
773-583-7884 or info@haymarketbooks.org.

This book was published with the generous support of Lannan Foundation
and the Wallace Action Fund.

Cover design by Eric Ruder.

Library of Congress Cataloging-in-Publication Data is available.

Printed in Canada by union labor.

10 9 8 7 6 5 4 3 2

"But what all the violence of the feudal institutions could never have effected, the silent and insensible operation of foreign commerce and manufactures brought about. These gradually furnished the great proprietors with something for which they could exchange the whole surplus produce of their lands, and which they could consume themselves without sharing it either with tenants or retainers. All for ourselves, and nothing for other people, seems, in every age of the world, to have been the vile maxim of the masters of mankind. As soon, therefore, as they could find a method of consuming the whole value of their rents themselves, they had no disposition to share them with any other persons."

—**Adam Smith**, *The Wealth of Nations*[1]

Table of Contents

Foreword

BY MARCUS RASKIN

Noam Chomsky's political activities and his understanding of the nature of language capacity may be described metaphorically as an unbroken band labeled *universality*. But his universality is no mystification aimed at masking truths and marginalizing truthful inquiries, nor is it the belief that all of public life must be the same everywhere. One side of the Chomsky strip is innateness, which presents humanity with the gift of language and therefore communication. Follow that strip of universality; you will note that there is imprinted on the strip a capacity that allows for rationality and moral action that can catalyze humanity's benign social purpose. We may even speculate that human nature contains a capacity for invariant empathy. We leap and conclude that humanity is more than a bunch of indivisible but empty monads unconnected except through their accidental collision; we further conclude that humankind is imprinted with an inexorable drive to create something better out of its raw material. We desire our shared knowledge to lead to love, and vice versa; we want power to be in service of both. Perhaps a humane world civilization might come into being in which universality does not assign a preferred place to any particular group, but in which all are joined in solidarity and mutual dignity with all others. However, when we look again we see that the strands of the strip are torn and they need repair.

But how to repair them so that the band does not disintegrate? What are the tools we use to repair the tear? And who repairs the band of which we are an integral part?

For Chomsky, in the deepest personal sense, language becomes a critical means for the repair of the tear(s) of humanity; the structure of language is a wondrous feature of life that is simultaneously stable and infinitely malleable. In this, his views are radically different from those of Jean-Paul Sartre, who sees words and language as keeping us from the world as it is, or perhaps could be. For Chomsky, there are two courses in attaining repair and in creating something different, a new thing, a new organizational structure or alternative. One is in the spoken and written word, which comes from how we are hardwired. The other is the language of exemplary doing, where general propositions, for example about love and empathy, are made clear in action through lived experience. In politics, the body and mind are the tools to repair the body and mind.

For the casual observer, Chomsky seems to hold that on the one hand, there is science and analysis, and on the other hand, there are those desired values that we hold dear and preach about through different social means. In this world, the body is divided into unconnected categories where mind and heart, thinking and discernment, are separate from emotions and feeling. Is this not what the modern academy attempted to create, hoping in this way to ensure a soundness and civility, a series of golden lies, the distance of self from object and therefore a perverted objectivity, thereby protecting the scientist and her inquiries while intentionally missing the point of integration and wholeness?

His fellow academics were in for a big surprise if they thought Chomsky was domesticated to accept rationality as a division between thinking, passion, and political commitment in terms of how one leads a life of responsibility. This supreme rationalist in his actions and studies says that the basic concerns of intellectuals must be "to speak the truth and expose lies."[1] For him the basic concern in the political realm is to integrate knowledge, power, and love as the basis of law and value. That is to say, the ideal intellectual is to exercise responsibility through his rationality and the exercise of courage and integrity to expose lies and to tell the truth. Human responsibility beyond a designated narrow social role can be a lonely activity in a society that gets by on grease paint and self-delusion. Chomsky's concern as a lover of wisdom that serves the wider humanity, as he knows and points out, can hit up against a stone wall where political thought and commentary is bereft of truth telling, even attempts at it.

It takes very little to find out what and whose interests are served when responsibility is defined in action as service to a master. Just spend a Sunday morning with the commentators on television whose interests have virtually nothing to do with truth telling and whose programs are sponsored by agribusiness and power companies. Responsibility morphs into servility. For many in the world of journalism and politics the consequences of what they do and why may not necessarily be known to them. The structure of Sunday morning news allows Exxon and a state apparatus to "guide" the journalist and the people listening. And this has dire consequences for a peaceful constitutional democracy. Read in Chomsky's *On Power and Ideology* the words of a columnist and former ambassador, William Shannon, who asserts that for the best of motives the United States ends up supporting military dictatorships, perhaps forgetting that everyone always claims the best of motives.[2] Throughout history American leaders have never shirked their responsibility of explaining in high-minded terms the American role in Asia, Africa, the Middle East, and Latin America. Politics is the means that tells us how we are going to arrange and use the mirrors of everyday life. It arranges the framework that turns "ought" into "is" in culture and experience. This is why practical actions, in the sense of choosing and responsibility, determine the course of human history.

This is why Chomsky's analysis and his practical actions are so important. They are the bellwether of *what could be.* His drive and commitment come from a directed use of passion, intuition, and a deeply held responsibility for others. It is what I have termed "standing with" or "withness." But withness is more than reporting to others. Withness takes us beyond personal interest, accepting the risks of the other when there is no "pragmatic" reason to do so. Withness is an instrument of awareness that helps us to know where and who we are, for it locates ourselves with others, and asks through example that others relocate and reorder themselves. When Henry David Thoreau, protesting the poll tax, was asked by Ralph Waldo Emerson, "Henry, why are you here?" Thoreau responded, "Waldo, why are you not here?"[3] There was no need for Chomsky to commit civil disobedience during the Indochina war except as a citizen responsibility. It was his statement of withness responsibility with the unseen Other. Our government could not respond to the anguish of millions; its policy makers were the chief culprits. If Chomsky's sensibility and drive were more infectious, it would be the saving possibility and hope of humanity. It would mean the recognition of international civil rights laws that renounced the color of legitimacy and would put an end to realpolitik from genocide to torture. It would mean an end to American military and economic imperialism; in the Indochina war, it would have meant a million lives saved. In the last decades, it would have meant that a quarter million Guatemalans would not have died with the not-so-silent assent of the United States.[4] It would mean that the United States would not supply with weapons and politically support the "stable oppression" seen throughout the Third World.[5]

Since in Chomsky's world the intellectual must turn his talent and spirit to the presentation of truthful accounts and acute analysis of things as they are, personal choices become obvious and inescapable. For Chomsky, inquiries are instruments that encourage the oppressed *to be free to do*. These inquiries mean seeing social relations and events without the opaque glasses considerately provided by closely interrelated universities, corporations, foundations, and media. On the intellectual side, rational inquiry seeks to "try to extract some principles that have explanatory force . . . thus hoping to account for at least the major effects."[6] This means analyzing how and to what end the United States organizes its clearly predominant global power.[7] With relatively free access to information, America's role in the world can be analyzed, explained, and understood with considerable accuracy.

But for Chomsky this is only half of the story. The question for him becomes "How does one live as an intellectual and citizen in the world of the dominant empire?" Now choices requiring courage emerge. They necessitate working against the grain of established conventional intellectuals who have surrendered their critical faculties and internalized the values of the hierarchic system, to an extent that they often do not even realize. While Chomsky and others, this writer included, may have contempt for the role of intellectual scribes such as Henry Kissinger, who organized the thoughts and interests of a ruling class so that it would feel more secure, condemnation must also extend to an educational and rewards system that is eager to turn out such scribes. Fabrication is the tool of the intellectual valet in the state apparatus; he or she dresses up force in perfumed clothes. This fabrication extends to institutions and "disciplines" that enforce and coordinate state and economic power.

Thus, Chomsky is not surprised by intellectuals and a professoriate whose interests in truthful, uncontrolled inquiry are relatively modest. Such inquiry would require personal risk, perceived jeopardy of status, and confrontation with authority. But how much risk to the intellectual is really involved? After all, the national security state clings to the ornamental trappings of constitutional democracy as long as they don't get in the way of power. For those in the middle class, the United States is not a totalitarian state within its own borders. Those who adopt a contrary or skeptical stance need not fear for their lives. Perhaps that is why Chomsky holds so many intellectuals in disdain. They really would risk little if they would act other than as clerks for power.

When Chomsky wonders in "The Responsibility of Intellectuals"[8] why Arthur Schlesinger Jr. lied on behalf of the Kennedy administration, and was then rewarded by the academic community with a distinguished chair at a university, he is talking as the preeminent scholar who hates fraud and cowardice. He disdains intellectuals who undermine the importance and value of intellectual honesty in order to retain a place at the palace court. In this sense, Chomsky challenges the intellectual's privileged place when he or she does not act as truth teller. For Chomsky, the intellectual has historic importance when acting as an outsider to established power. Rationality allows us to demystify social constructions and find discernible messages that lay the basis for understanding and action. It is here where the meaning of language is turned into moral action. It is here that Chomsky has chosen to show by words, lived experiences, and acts what he has in mind. Throughout the essays in *The Masters of Mankind*, Chomsky raises moral and legal questions about responsibility and accountability, as well as the meaning of rights embedded in law. Indeed, what does it mean to be responsible in relation to moral acts?

Chomsky knows full well the limits of leaders and of their advisors, the arrogance, posturing, and malign intentions he finds in their words. It does not matter whether these leaders are elected or appointed, or hold their office through blood or advantage of wealth or even as the result of some level of educational attainment useful to a ruling elite. He is aware that oligarchs do not rule as trustees for others, but for themselves. They have in mind the destruction of democracy if it ever proves to be more than a rhetorical fig leaf, when it means the redistribution of economic and political power along the ideological lines of Adam Smith and Tom Paine, or when it means the renunciation of imperialism. There is a direct line between the antidemocratic elites and the establishment of secret organizations such as the CIA, which know and do things that a democracy would not begin to understand or countenance—until the democracy is deadened through propaganda. The history of the American struggle with elitism is, of course, embedded in the Constitution and Declaration of Independence. The Electoral College, the establishment of secret agencies, and the limit of two senators per state are examples of fearing the people.

This problem became even more acute during the Cold War when the United States inherited and strove for imperial expansion. Whether it was the elitism of Walter Lippmann or the pipe-smoking spymaster Allen Dulles, secrets were deemed necessary against the public that needed "embedded" journalists to interpret reality for them. Chomsky is aware of the difficulties of concretizing ideals in practice, finding that what is propounded is not the same as what can be accommodated and accepted in practice. But even more so, he is aware of the structures and policies that patently lead in antidemocratic directions, where the rhetoric of democracy and freedom is a self-serving mask for decidedly unlovely consequences.

The imperial brand of globalism that emanates from the Pentagon and Wall Street is an example of oligarchy posing as the spread of democracy. Economically, poor nations are treated to a burlesque of Adam Smith's ideas of a free market while in reality being burdened by colonialism and neocolonialism. More importantly, they bring into being the distortion and degradation of human possibility. Globalism in its present form is the organization of immiseration through technology and imperialism. Under corporate globalism, the humane and political potentiality of the person is turned into a bundle of unrequited desires answered only by deplorable working and living conditions.

Yet Chomsky must believe that technology and communication could be fused to create the possibility of a world civilization. Surely this must have been one of the attractions of being at MIT, that factory for the pushing of possible worlds into reality. In that milieu he witnesses a new set of relationships emerging beyond the nation-state that perhaps could give rise in the twenty-first century to anarcracies. They would be bound together by a vast interlocking communications network that could yield the creation of a world civilization with plural cultures and without the burden of the nation-state. It could be a world in which differences in principles and ways of living could bang against one another through analysis and discussion, clarifying and deepening understanding, leading to more general principles that uncover and reflect that innate capacity for decency found in people and reflected in common documents such as the Universal Declaration of Human Rights. It is the human tragedy that these documents only seem to arise after great upheavals. They do have political weight once they come into being. They are reinterpreted through an intermingling of law and violent and nonviolent action—as, say, in the liberation of South Africa from apartheid, the moral force of the successful civil rights struggles within the United States, and the successful attempts at confronting military imperialism in and over the Third World. These struggles have led to attitudes and assumptions of scholarship as we learn more about ourselves through the quest for common enduring principles intended to liberate humanity.

Even if it is misplaced moral fervor or Machiavellian cleverness justifying the use of overwhelming force, that language of justification becomes the basis upon which succeeding generations build their struggles for expanded human rights. The oppressed ask, "If freedom and justice apply to oligarchs, why can't they apply to us?" Chomsky understands that law itself has two aspects. One is the politics and power struggles of the past frozen into rituals, laws, and court decisions, the conclusions of which are reified and laid onto the future: law as restraint that from time to time needs direct challenge. In this sense, the civil disobedience actions that Chomsky undertook as a conscientious citizen (with his Hush Puppies and book bag) were meant as a way to reshape the law, seeing it less as the consensus between competing powerful and often unaccountable interests or prejudices written in legal language, and more as law in a second sense, as the basis upon which civilization must function. Law and lawmakers need a nudge to arrive at a level of respect for freedom and dignity—concepts linked in Chomsky's political actions—so that law advances society to its next stage of freedom. Law in the hands of judges who take seriously the Bill of Rights and the preamble to the Constitution, as well as other foundational documents, takes on that meritorious purpose. It organizes a set of rituals and words that reflect the inquiry and actions of dignity and liberation. It seeks to influence practice constituted as extending freedom and holding at bay the dogs of oppression and war. Thus, the task of the "jurisprude" is the setting of new boundaries, internalizing the spirit of freedom in those boundaries so that they become more than Sunday school rhetoric. They are guides based on felt injustice and inquiry. Or, to stick with our metaphor, they are the threads of the Möbius strip that may or may not be seen but are recognized and repaired through our actions and those of our social and legal structures.

A new generation might ask whether the positive features of enlightenment can be used and expanded in this century. I suspect Chomsky might say yes in more optimistic moments. For there is within human nature the capacity for betterment, empathy, and active caring. This nature can be fulfilled through our reason and those feelings that Mikhail Kropotkin described at the beginning of the twentieth century that would lead to wholly different but not utopian institutions. After all, Chomsky shows in these essays and in his body of work that practical paths can be found without demanding sainthood from each person. Rather he tells us that political action tied to demystification and analysis clears a path through the underbrush of mistakes and lies. Chomsky has acted as the wise catalyst for this necessary purpose. His thought and actions have made an indelible mark on two generations, and no doubt will do so for generations to come. In another time and in another tradition, we might have said that Chomsky's focused energy derived from a religious calling, a comment that Chomsky would surely scoff at and reject. His mastery of public texts is as awesome as scholars who analyze and interpret the words of the Talmud. His commitment to truth and justice is no less a religious calling than Reinhold Niebuhr's was to the idea of the Christian God as the hope of humankind, and without the muddle-headed contradictions that Niebuhr offered as practical guides to the perplexed and the opportunistic.

In Plato's *Republic,* Socrates expresses great fear about democracy because it is, in his mind, synonymous with freedom. The result is tyranny. But modern times have brought us a different understanding of democracy as an ideal. It is how to give the appearance of democracy yet deny it in practice, ensuring that democracy in its false form gives consent by the people to a small group, the oligarchs. This is accomplished through a combination of the people's silence and a rigged system that changes a working democracy of public participation and deliberation to a charade. In his essay "Consent Without Consent" in this volume, Chomsky exposes for us what all should know, but that the middle class, if it is doing well, has a tendency to forget: the two major political parties are business-oriented parties identifying in their soul with the centrality of big corporations as the engine of American life. Of course, in the workplace standards have always been rock solid. There is to be no kidding around about democracy. The workplace is the very definition of top-down authoritarianism. In this case, labor and the union movement have been in a continuous struggle around how deeply authoritarianism can extend into the lives of the workers—not whether it should exist. The business classes are forever conscious of class struggle and the importance of winning it.

Chomsky has not been alone in understanding the nature of class struggle and the baleful effects of a greedy oligarchy. Tom Paine understood the American Revolution as the struggle over democracy and the need of the people to judge, participate, and deliberate on their own destiny. Even James Madison, who best reflected the melding of aristocracy and republic as the way to ensure stability and to keep the barbarians away from power, was shocked to find that the real barbarians were sitting inside, not outside, the gate. In the twentieth century, John Dewey understood that those who held the keys to production, distribution, publicity, and transportation arrogated to themselves the role of rulers of the country. We may go one step further. The oligarchic national security state has turned the public election system into a wholly ornamental activity that we might term "politainment," politics as entertainment. Given control over the public discourse, it is relatively easy to change the channel of concern, changing the "discourse" like a child who might otherwise be caught out in a lie. This skill should not be underestimated and is really part of the genius of American advertising and state propaganda.

A large part of US history, like that of other nations, can be read as a narrative of imperial hubris.[9] But in every case there were also individuals who argued with and confronted this hubris. Chomsky is one of them.

ONE

Knowledge and Power: Intellectuals and the Welfare-Warfare State*

"War is the health of the State," wrote Randolph Bourne in a classic essay as America entered the First World War:

> It automatically sets in motion throughout society those irresistible forces for uniformity, for passionate cooperation with the Government in coercing into obedience the minority groups and individuals which lack the larger herd sense. . . . Other values such as artistic creation, knowledge, reason, beauty, the enhancement of life, are instantly and almost unanimously sacrificed, and the significant classes who have constituted themselves the amateur agents of the State are engaged not only in sacrificing these values for themselves but in coercing all other persons into sacrificing them.

And at the service of society's "significant classes" were the intelligentsia, "trained up in the pragmatic dispensation, immensely ready for the executive ordering of events, pitifully unprepared for the intellectual interpretation or the idealistic focusing of ends." They are: "lined up in service of the war-technique. There seems to have been a peculiar congeniality between the war and these men. It is as if the war and they had been waiting for each other."[1]

---

*From "Knowledge and Power: Intellectuals and the Welfare-Warfare State," in *The New Left*, ed. Priscilla Long (Boston: Porter Sargent, 1970), pp. 172–99.

Bourne emphasizes the ideological consequences of national mobilization: the "irresistible forces for uniformity" that induce obedience to the State and subservience to the needs of the "significant classes." To this we may add the material benefits of mobilization for war, particularly evident in World War II and the Cold War as government intervention in the economy brought the depression to a close and guaranteed the "healthy functioning" of an economy geared, quite extensively, to the social goals of destruction and waste. Events have verified Bourne's prediction that the mobilization for war would bring the intelligentsia to a position of power and influence "in the service of the war technique." His remarks may be compared to those of James Thomson, East Asian specialist at the Department of State and the White House between 1961 and 1966:

> [T]he increased commitment to Vietnam was also fueled by a new breed of military strategists and academic social scientists (some of whom had entered the new Administration) who had developed theories of counterguerrilla warfare and were eager to see them put to the test. To some, "counterinsurgency" seemed a new panacea for coping with the world's instability. . . . There is a result of our Vietnam policy which holds potential danger for the future of American foreign policy: *the rise of a new breed of American ideologues who see Vietnam as the ultimate test of their doctrine.* . . . In a sense, these men are our counterpart to the visionaries of communism's radical left: they are technocracy's own Maoists. They do not govern Washington today—but their doctrine rides high.[2]

To this observation we can conjoin another, regarding a parallel phenomenon that has been the subject of wide discussion in recent years: "Power in economic life has over time passed from its ancient association with land to association with capital and then on, in recent times, to the composite of knowledge and skills which comprises the technostructure . . . [that is, the group that] embraces all who bring specialized knowledge, talent or experience to group decision-making [in government and corporation]."[3]

The role of the technical intelligentsia in decision-making is predominant in those parts of the economy that are "in the service of the war technique" (or such substitutes as the space race) and that are closely linked to government, which underwrites their security and growth. It is little wonder, then, that the technical intelligentsia is, typically, committed to what Barrington Moore calls "the predatory solution of token reform at home and counterrevolutionary imperialism abroad."[4] Elsewhere, Moore offers the following summary of the "predominant voice of America at home and abroad"—an ideology that expresses the needs of the American socioeconomic elite, that is propounded with various gradations of subtlety by many American intellectuals, and that gains substantial adherence on the part of the majority that has obtained "some share in the affluent society":

> You may protest in words as much as you like. There is but one condition attached to the freedom we would very much like to encourage: your protests may be as loud as possible as long as they remain ineffective. Though we regret your sufferings very much and would like to do something about them—indeed we have studied them very carefully and have already spoken to your rulers and immediate superiors about these matters—any attempt by you to remove your oppressors by force is a threat to civilized society and the democratic process. Such threats we cannot and shall not tolerate. As you resort to force, we will, if need be, wipe you from the face of the earth by the measured response that rains down flame from the skies.[5]

A society in which this is the predominant voice can be maintained only through some form of national mobilization, which may range in its extent from, at the minimum, a commitment of substantial resources to a credible threat of force and violence. Given the realities of international politics, this commitment can be maintained in the United States only by a form of national psychosis of the sort given voice, for example, by the present secretary of defense, who sees us "locked in a real war, joined in mortal combat on the battlefield, each contender maneuvering for advantage"[6]—a war against an enemy who appears in many guises: Kremlin bureaucrat, Asian peasant, Latin American student, and, no doubt, "urban guerrilla" at home. Far saner voices can be heard expressing a perception that is not totally dissimilar.[7] Perhaps success can be attained in the national endeavor announced by this predominant voice.

In Moore's informed judgment, the system "has considerable flexibility and room for maneuver, including strategic retreat."[8] In any event, this much is fairly sure. Success can be achieved only at the cost of severe demoralization, which will make life as meaningless for those who share in the affluent society as it is hopeless for the peasant in Guatemala. Perhaps "war is the health of the state"—but only in the sense in which an economy is "healthy" when a rising GNP includes the cost of napalm and missiles and riot-control devices, jails and detention camps, placing a man on the moon, and so on.

Even in this sense of "health," it is not war that is the health of the state in the modern era, but rather permanent preparation for war. Full-scale war means that the game is lost. Even a "limited war" can be harmful, not only to the economy,[9] as the stock market and the complaints of aerospace executives indicate, but also to the long-range commitment to the use of force. Probably what success the peace movement has had in limiting the attack on Vietnam came not from its present power but rather from the danger that the "predominant voice" that Moore correctly hears might be challenged in a more general and far-reaching way. Better to nip dissent in the bud while it is still focused on the specific atrocity of Vietnam and deflect a movement that might, if it grows, begin to raise serious questions about American society and its international role. Thus we now hear of the mistake of bombing North Vietnam (which caused moral outrage and thus threatened the stability of the body politic)[10] and of using conscripts to fight a colonial war; and we hear proposals for a volunteer army at "market prices" so that resistance will be cooled when Vietnam is reenacted elsewhere.

I would like to elaborate on both of Bourne's points: the function of preparation for war in guaranteeing the health of the state, and the opportunities that this condition provides for "the new breed of American ideologues"—adding some historical perspective and some comments on what intellectuals might hope to do to counter these tendencies.

The intellectual has, traditionally, been caught between the conflicting demands of truth and power. He would like to see himself as the man who seeks to discern the truth, to tell the truth as he sees it, to act—collectively where he can, alone where he must—to oppose injustice and oppression, to help bring a better social order into being. If he chooses this path, he can expect to be a lonely creature, disregarded or reviled. If, on the other hand, he brings his talents to the service of power, he can achieve prestige and affluence. He may also succeed in persuading himself—perhaps, on occasion, with justice—that he can humanize the exercise of power by the "significant classes." He may hope to join with them or even replace them in the role of social management, in the ultimate interest of efficiency and freedom. The intellectual who aspires to this role may use the rhetoric of revolutionary socialism or of welfare-state social engineering in pursuit of his vision of a "meritocracy" in which knowledge and technical ability confer power. He may represent himself as part of a "revolutionary vanguard" leading the way to a new society or as a technical expert applying "piecemeal technology" to the management of a society that can meet its problems without fundamental changes. For some, the choice may depend on little more than an assessment of the relative strength of competing social forces. It comes as no surprise, then, that quite commonly the roles shift; the student radical becomes the counterinsurgency expert. His claims must, in either case, be viewed with suspicion: he is propounding the self-serving ideology of a "meritocratic elite" that, in Marx's phrase (applied, in this case, to the bourgeoisie), defines "the special conditions of its emancipation [as] the *general* conditions through which alone modern society can be saved." Failure to present a reasoned justification will simply confirm these suspicions.

Long ago, Kropotkin observed that "the modern radical is a centralizer, a State partisan, a Jacobin to the core, and the Socialist walks in his footsteps."[11] To a large extent he is correct in thus echoing the warning of Bakunin that "scientific socialism" might in practice be distorted into "the despotic domination of the laboring masses by a new aristocracy, small in number, composed of real or pretended experts,"[12] the "red bureaucracy" that would prove to be "the most vile and terrible lie that our century has created."[13] Western critics have been quick to point out how the Bolshevik leadership took on the role outlined in the anarchist critique[14]—as was in fact sensed by Rosa Luxemburg,[15] barely a few months before her murder by the troops of the German socialist government exactly half a century ago.

Rosa Luxemburg's critique of Bolshevism was sympathetic and fraternal but incisive, and full of meaning for today's radical intellectuals. Fourteen years earlier, in her *Leninism or Marxism*,[16] she had criticized Leninist organizational principles, arguing that *"nothing will more surely enslave a young labor movement to an intellectual elite hungry for power than this bureaucratic straitjacket, which will immobilize the movement and turn it into an automaton manipulated by a Central Committee."* These dangerous tendencies toward authoritarian centralization she saw, with great accuracy, in the earliest stages of the Bolshevik revolution. She examined the conditions that led the Bolshevik leadership to terror and dictatorship of "a little leading minority in the name of the class," a dictatorship that stifled "the growing political training of the mass of the people" instead of contributing to it; and she warned against making a virtue of necessity and turning authoritarian practice into a style of rule by the new elite. Democratic institutions have their defects: "But the remedy which Trotsky and Lenin[17] have found, the elimination of democracy as such, is worse than the disease it is supposed to cure; for it stops up the very living source from which alone can come the correction of all the innate shortcomings of social institutions. That source is the active, untrammeled, energetic political life of the broadest masses of the people."

Unless the whole mass of the people take part in the determination of all aspects of economic and social life, unless the new society grows out of their creative experience and spontaneous action, it will be merely a new form of repression. "Socialism will be decreed from behind a few official desks by a dozen intellectuals," whereas in fact it "demands a complete spiritual transformation in the masses degraded by centuries of bourgeois class rule," a transformation that can take place only within institutions that extend the freedoms of bourgeois society. There is no explicit recipe for socialism: "Only experience is capable of correcting and opening new ways. Only unobstructed, effervescing life falls into a thousand new forms and improvisations, brings to light creative force, itself corrects all mistaken attempts."

The role of the intellectuals and radical activists, then, must be to assess and evaluate, to attempt to persuade, to organize, but not to seize power and rule. "Historically, the errors committed by a truly revolutionary movement are infinitely more fruitful than the infallibility of the cleverest Central Committee."[18]

These remarks are a useful guide for the radical intellectual. They also provide a refreshing antidote to the dogmatism so typical of discourse on the left, with its arid certainties and religious fervor regarding matters that are barely understood—the self-destructive left-wing counterpart to the smug superficiality of the defenders of the status quo who can perceive their own ideological commitments no more than a fish can perceive that it swims in the sea.

It would be useful, though beyond the bounds of discussion, to review the interplay between radical intellectuals and technical intelligentsia on the one hand and mass, popular-based organizations on the other, in revolutionary and post-revolutionary situations. Such an investigation might consider at one extreme the Bolshevik experience and the ideology of the liberal technocracy, which are united in the belief that mass organizations and popular politics must be submerged.[19] At the other extreme, it might deal with the anarchist revolution in Spain in 1936–37—and the response to it by liberal and Communist intellectuals.[20] Equally relevant would be the evolving relationship between the Communist Party and the popular organizations (workers' councils and commune governments) in Yugoslavia today,[21] and the love-hate relationship between party cadres and peasant associations that provides the dramatic tension for William Hinton's brilliant account of a moment in the Chinese revolution.[22] It could draw from the experience of the National Liberation Front as described, say, by Douglas Pike in his *Vietcong*[23] and other more objective sources,[24] and from many documentary accounts of developments in Cuba. One should not exaggerate the relevance of these cases to the problems of an advanced industrial society, but I think there is no doubt that a great deal can nevertheless be learned from them, not only about the feasibility of other forms of social organization[25] but also about the problems that arise as intellectuals and activists attempt to relate to mass politics.

It is worth mention that the post–World War I remnants of the non-Bolshevik left reechoed and sharpened the critique of the "revolutionary vanguard" of activist intellectuals. The Dutch Marxist Anton Pannekoek[26] describes "the aim of the Communist Party—which it called world-revolution" in this way: "to bring to power, by means of the fighting force of the workers, a layer of leaders who then establish planned production by means of State Power." Continuing:

> The social ideals growing up in the minds of the intellectual class now that it feels its increasing importance in the process of production: a well-ordered organization of production for use under the direction of technical and scientific experts—are hardly different [from those of the Bolshevik leadership]. So the Communist Party considers this class its natural allies which it has to draw into its circle. By an able theoretical propaganda it tries to detach the intelligentsia from the spiritual influences of the declining bourgeoisie and of private capitalism, and to win them for the revolution that will put them into their proper place as a new leading and ruling class . . . they will intervene and slide themselves in as leaders of the revolution, nominally to give their aid by taking part in the fight, in reality to deflect the action in the direction of their party aims. Whether or not the beaten bourgeoisie will then rally with them to save of capitalism what can be saved, in any case their intervention comes down to cheating the workers, leading them off from the road to freedom. . . . The Communist Party, though it may lose ground among the workers, tries to form with the socialists and the intellectual class a united front, ready at the first major crisis of capitalism to take in its hands the power over and against the workers. . . . Thus the fighting working class, basing itself upon Marxism, will find Lenin's philosophical work a stumbling-block in its way, as the theory of a class that tries to perpetuate its serfdom.[27]

And in the postwar Western welfare state, the technically trained intelligentsia also aspire to positions of control in the emerging state-capitalist societies in which a powerful state is linked in complex ways to a network of corporations that are on their way to becoming international institutions. They look forward to "a well-ordered production for use under the direction of technical scientific experts" in what they describe as the "post-industrial technetronic society" in which "plutocratic pre-eminence comes under a sustained challenge from the political leadership which itself is increasingly permeated by individuals possessing special skills and intellectual talents," a society in which "knowledge becomes a tool of power, and the effective mobilization of talent an important way for acquiring power."[28]

Bourne's critical words on the treachery of the intellectuals thus fall within a broader analytic framework. Furthermore, his perception of the ideological role of the mobilization for war has been proven accurate by events. When Bourne wrote, the United States was already the world's major industrial society—in the 1890s, its industrial production already equaled that of the United Kingdom, France, and Germany combined.[29] The war of course greatly enhanced its position of economic superiority. From World War II, the United States emerged as the world-dominant power, and so it has remained. The national mobilization for war permitted the exercise of means to escape from the economic stagnation of the 1930s and provided some important insights into economics. As Chandler puts it:

> World War II taught other lessons. The government spent far more than the most enthusiastic New Dealer had ever proposed. Most of the output of the expenditures was destroyed or left on the battlefields of Europe and Asia. But the resulting increased demand sent the nation into a period of prosperity the like of which had never before been seen. Moreover, the supplying of huge armies and navies fighting the most massive war of all time required a tight, centralized control of the national economy. This effort brought corporate managers to Washington to carry out one of the most complex pieces of economic planning in history. That experience lessened the ideological fears over the government's role in stabilizing the economy.[30]

Apparently, the lesson was learned very well. It has been pointed out, accurately, that in the postwar world "the armaments industry has provided a sort of automatic stabilizer for the whole economy,"[31] and enlightened corporate managers, far from fearing government intervention in the economy, view "the New Economics as a technique for increasing corporate viability."[32]

The ensuing Cold War carried further the depoliticization of American society and created a psychological environment in which the government was able to intervene, in part through fiscal policies, public works, and public services, but very largely through "defense" spending, as "a coordinator of last resort" when "managers are unable to maintain a high level of aggregate demand" (Chandler). The Cold War has also guaranteed the financial resources as well as the psychological environment for the government to undertake an extensive commitment to the project of constructing an integrated world economy dominated by American capital—"no idealistic pipe dream," according to George Ball, "but a hard-headed prediction; it is a role into which we are being pushed by the imperatives of our own technology."[33] The major instrument is the multinational corporation, described by Ball as follows: "In its modern form, the multinational corporation, or one with world-wide operations and markets, is a distinctly American development. Through such corporations it has become possible for the first time to use the world's resources with maximum efficiency. . . . But there must be greater unification of the world economy to give full play to the benefits of multinational corporations."[34]

The multinational corporation itself is the beneficiary of the mobilization of resources by the government, and its activities are backed, ultimately, by American military force. Simultaneously, there is a process of increased centralization of control in the domestic economy, as also in political life, with the decline of parliamentary institutions—a decline that is, in fact, noticeable throughout the Western industrial societies.[35]

The "unification of the world economy" by American-based international corporations obviously poses serious threats to freedom. The Brazilian political economist Helio Jaguaribe, no radical, puts it as follows:

> Increasing dependence on alien developed countries, particularly the United States, together with increasing internal poverty and unrest, would leave the Latin American peoples with the choice between permanent foreign domination and internal revolution. This alternative is already visible in the Caribbean area, where the countries have lost their individual viability and are not being allowed, by the combined action of their own internal oligarchies and the external intervention of the United States, to form a larger autonomous

community. What is happening today in the Caribbean is likely to happen in less than two decades in the major Latin American countries if they do not achieve minimal conditions of autonomous self-sustained development.[36]

It is no secret that the same concerns arise in Asia, and even in Western Europe, where national capital is incapable of competing with state-supported American enterprise, the system that Nieburg describes as "a government-subsidized private profit system."[37]

Economic domination carries with it as well the threat of cultural subjugation—not a threat but a positive virtue, from the point of view of the colonial administrator or, often, the American political scientist delighted with the opportunity to preside over the "modernization" of some helpless society. An example, extreme perhaps, is the statement of an American diplomat in Laos: "For this country, it is necessary, in order to achieve any progress, to level everything. It is necessary to reduce the inhabitants to zero, to disencumber them of their traditional culture which blocks everything."[38]

At another level, the same phenomenon can be observed in Latin America. Claude Julien comments:

> The revolt of Latin American students is not directed only against dictatorial regimes that are corrupt and inefficient—nor only against the exploitation by the foreigner of the economic and human resources of their country—but also against the cultural colonization that touches them at the deepest level of their being. And this is perhaps why their revolt is more virulent than that of the worker or peasant organizations that experience primarily economic colonization.[39]

The classic case in the American empire is the Philippines, where the effects have been disastrous.

The long-range threat is to national independence and cultural vitality, as well as to successful, balanced economic development.[40] The factors interweave. Domestic ruling elites develop a vested interest in American dominance and even in American imperial ventures—a fact illustrated clearly in the Far East, where the Korean war and now the Vietnam war have substantially contributed to the "health" of the states that are gradually being "unified" in the American system. At times the results verge on the grotesque: thus Japan produces the plastic containers used to ship home corpses of American soldiers, and "the successor companies to I. G. Farben, the firm which produced Zyklon B for the gas chambers of the German extermination camps, . . . have now set up an industrial plant in South Vietnam for the production of toxic chemicals and gases for the US expeditionary force."[41] The ordinary reality is grim enough, without such examples.

Each year in the Economic Survey of Asia and the Pacific published by the *New York Times* we read such items as this:

> *Thais See Peace as a Mixed Blessing*: . . . [It is an] unarguable fact that an end to the fighting [in Vietnam] would pose a grave threat to Thailand's economy. *The Investor*, the new monthly magazine of the Thai Board of Investment, put the case candidly in the cover story of its first issue, published in December. "The economic development of Thailand has become so inextricably linked with the war," the magazine said, "that whatever decisions the United States makes about its future role in Southeast Asia cannot fail to have far reaching implications here." "An abrupt termination of the American war effort in Southeast Asia," the magazine went on to say, "would be quite painful economically". . . . If, however, as many people think, an American pullout from Vietnam actually results in an even bigger United States military presence here, the Thais will be faced with the even more difficult choice between a continued boom and further deterioration of their traditional society.[42]

The impact is severe, and cumulative: it is added to the devastating heritage of the colonial era, nicely summarized, for example, in the testimony of the director of the USAID Mission in the Philippines before a House subcommittee on April 25, 1967:

> Agriculture . . . is a product of almost studied neglect—inadequate transportation, limited irrigation, insufficient farm credit programs, price policies aimed at cheap food for urban areas which discourage farm production, high rate of tenancy, absentee land ownership, poorly organized markets and high interest rates. The average farmer (with a family of six) in Central Luzon makes about 800 pesos from his farming operation. His condition has not changed in the last fifty years [to

be more precise, since the Spanish occupation]. Perhaps even more critical than the actual condition of the rural inhabitant . . . is the ever increasing gap between urban and rural living. . . . In the past ten years the rich have become richer and the poor have become poorer.[43]

Conceivably new technical advances—for example, "miracle rice"—may help. One certainly hopes so, but the advance euphoria seems questionable:

The new high-yielding varieties, developed partly by Ford- and Rockefeller-financed organizations, require scientific management, two to three times the cash inputs previously needed, and extensive water control. . . . [If self-sufficiency is reached], the market price of the commodity will drop considerably in the Philippines. This means that only the most efficient farming units will lie with the large, mechanized, tenantless, agro-business farms. This technological fact, coupled with a loophole in the Land Reform Code that allows a land-lord to throw his tenants off the land and retain it himself if he farms the area, might destroy whatever attempts are made at land reform in the Philippines. . . . [President Marcos] is very much aware of a little-publicized report issued in 1965, which clearly proves the feu-dal, and therefore explosive, nature of Philippine rural society. The report reveals that only eighteen years ago, less than half of 1 percent of the population owned 42 percent of the agricultural land. Two hundred and twenty-one of the largest landowners—the Catholic Church being the largest—held over 9 percent of the farm area. In 1958, nearly 50 percent of the farmers were tenants and an additional 20 percent of the farmers were tenants and an additional 20 percent were farm laborers. Thus 70 percent of those employed in agriculture were landless. . . . In 1903, the tenancy rate for the entire country was 18 percent excluding farm laborers. By 1948 this figure had climbed to 37 percent. In 1961, it was over 50 percent. There is no evidence that this trend has at all changed in the last eight years. It may even be outpacing the minuscule efforts at land reform. . . . Will the Con-gress in Manila, composed of the very same rural banking elite, ever vote the necessary funds to finance the Agricultural Credit Admin-istration, the Land Bank and Cooperatives?[44]

The report may have gone on to indicate that this situation is, largely, a consequence of American colonial policy, and it also might have ven-tured a prediction as to the fate of those driven off the land under "rationalization" in a country that has been described as an American vegetable garden.

Similar reports are coming from India: "Though it is clear that the Indian farmer wants to exploit the new technology, it is less clear that he has been able to do so to any dramatic degree in the paddy fields."[45] The same report cites another problem, namely: "State governments in India have been eliminating taxes on the incomes of the more prosperous farmers at a time when those incomes have been rising steadily. Politicians are convinced that it would be suicidal for any party to press for the restoration of these taxes. But without some mechanism for diverting a portion of the new income in rural areas to development, growth will inevitably lag."

Again, this situation is a legacy of colonialism. It can be met only by social reconstruction of a sort that, throughout the world, will now be resisted by American influence and direct application of force, the latter applied, where possible, through the medium of the American-trained and -equipped native armies. Brazil is merely the most recent and most obvious example. There, the military elite preaches this ideology: "Accepting the principle of 'total war against subversion,' the doctrine of national security considers that the 'underdeveloped countries must aid the leading State of the Christian world to defend civilization by furnishing it with primary materials.'"[46]

In such ways, it becomes possible, to return to George Ball's formulation, "to use the world's resources with maximum efficiency" and with "greater unification of the world economy." In such ways we strive to realize the prediction outlined long ago by Brooks Adams: "Our geographical position, our wealth, and our energy preeminently fit us to enter upon the development of Eastern Asia [but why only there?] and to reduce it to part of our own economic system."[47] Our own economic system, meanwhile, is heavily dependent on government-induced production. Increasingly, it is becoming a "government-subsidized private profit system" with a deep involvement of the technical intelligentsia. The system is tolerated by public opinion, which is tortured by chimeras and stupefied by the mass media.

That a situation such as this is fraught with perils is obvious. From the point of view of the liberal technocrat the solution to the problem lies in strengthening the federal government (the "radical centralizer" goes further, insisting that all power be vested in the central state authorities and the "vanguard party"). Only thus can the military-industrial complex be tamed and controlled: "The filter-down process of pump-priming the civilian economy by fostering ever-greater economic concentration and income inequality must be replaced by a frank acceptance of federal responsibility to control the tide of economic bigness, and to plan the conservation and growth of all sectors of the economy and the society."[48]

The hope lies in skilled managers such as Robert McNamara, who "has been the unflinching hero of the campaign to reform and control the 'Contract State.'"[49] It is probably correct to suppose that the technostructure offers no greater hope than McNamara, who has clearly explained his own views regarding social organization: "Vital decision-making, in policy matters as well as in business, must remain at the top. This is partly—though not completely—what the top is for."

Ultimate control must be vested in the hands of management, which is, "in the end, the most creative of all the arts—for its medium is human talent itself." This is apparently a divine imperative: "God is clearly democratic. He distributes brainpower universally. But He quite justifiably expects us to do something efficient and constructive with that priceless gift. That is what management is all about."[50]

This is a relatively pure form of the vision of the technocratic elite. We can arrive at a more considered judgment regarding the likely role of a strengthened federal authority in a state capitalist society by examining the past record. The federal government has continuously accelerated the arms race and the centralization of the domestic and international economy, not only by subsidizing research and development, but also by investment that is turned over to private capital and by direct purchase.[51] A plausible forecast is suggested by Letwin's observation that in the past, "businessmen invented, advocated, or at least rapidly recognized the usefulness of each main measure of [government intervention]" since they could thus "put government to positive use as a means for imposing the social arrangements that suited their own economic interests." McNamara's capitulation on the ABM system, in the face of his clear understanding of its irrationality (except as a subsidy to the electronics industry) indicates rather dramatically what the more human forces among the technical intelligentsia can hope to achieve solely by "working from within."

As we move into the Nixon period, there is every reason to suppose that even the feeble gestures of the McNamaras will be restrained. In a series of articles in the *Washington Post* (December 1968), Bernard Nossiter quotes the president of North American Rockwell: "All of Mr. Nixon's statements on weapons and space are very positive. I think he has perhaps a little more awareness of these things than some people we've seen in the White House." The above prospect, Nossiter concludes from his study, is this:

> Powerful industrial giants eagerly pressing for more military business, Pentagon defense planners eager to get on with the new weapons production, Congressmen whose districts profit directly from the anticipated contracts, and millions of Americans from the blue collar aircraft worker to the university physicist drawing their paychecks from the production of arms. About to take over the White House is a new president whose campaign left little doubt of his inclination to support the ABM and other costly arms spending while tightening up on expenditures for civilian purposes. This is the military-industrial complex of 1969.

Of course, any competent economist can sketch other methods by which government-induced production can serve to keep the economy functioning. "But capitalist reality is more intractable than planners' pens and paper. For one thing too much productive expenditure by the state is ruled out. Seen from the individual capitalist's corner, such expenditure would be a straight invasion of his preserve by an immensely more powerful and materially resourceful competitor; as such it needs to be fought off."[52]

Furthermore, in a society in which a "vigorous appetite for income and wealth" is extolled as the highest good (see note 50), it is difficult—subversive of the prevailing ideology, in fact—to mobilize popular support for use of the resources for the public welfare or to meet human needs, however desperate they may be. The point is explained clearly by Samuel F. Downer, financial vice president for LTV aerospace, who is quoted by Nossiter in explanation of why "the post-war world must be bolstered with military orders": "It's basic. Its selling appeal is defense of the home. This is one of the greatest appeals the politicians have to adjusting the system. If you're President and you need a central factor in the economy, and you need to sell this factor, you can't sell Harlem and Watts but you can sell self-preservation, a new environment. We're going to increase defense budgets as long as those Russians are ahead of us. The American people understand this."

Similarly, the American people "understand" the necessity for the grotesquerie of the space race, which is quite susceptible to Madison Avenue techniques and thus, along with the science-technology race in general, serves as "a transfigured, transmuted and theoretical substitute for an infinite strategic arms race; it is a continuation of the race by other means."[53] It is fashionable to decry such analyses—or even references to the "military-industrial complex"—as "unsophisticated." It is interesting, therefore, to note that those who manipulate the process and stand directly to gain by it are much less coy about the matter.

There are some perceptive analysts—J. K. Galbraith is the best example—who argue that the concern for growth and profit maximization has become only one of several motives for management and technostructure, that it is supplemented, perhaps dominated, by identification with and adaptation to the needs of the organization, the corporation, which serves as a basic planning unit for the economy.[54] Perhaps this is true, but the consequences of this shift of motivation may nevertheless be slight, since the corporation as planning unit is geared to production of consumer goods[55]—the consumer, often, being the national state—rather than satisfaction of social needs, and to the extension of its dominion in the organized international economy.

In his famous address on the military-industrial complex, President Eisenhower warned that: "The prospect of domination of the nation's scholars by Federal employment, project allocations, and the power of money is ever present—and is gravely to be regarded." In fact, the government has long been the "employer of last resort"—in fact, the dominant employer—for the engineering profession, and there is little doubt that the world would be a better place without a good deal of the technology that is being developed.

The facts are clearly perceived and rightly deplored by many very able critics. H. L. Neiburg, in the work cited, explains the background for the "science-technology race" as follows: "Built into this equation and secondary to it is the need to maintain a healthy economy. Fear of stagnation, the habit of massive wartime spending, the vested interests embracing virtually all groups, pork-barrel politics—all are aspects of what has become deliberate government policy to invest in the 'research and development' empire as an economic stimulant and a public works project."

He shows how government contracts have become "an escape route" from the "stagnating civilian economy," with the "contemporary dedication to science" and the "popular faith in the mystique of innovation" serving as "a cover for the emergence of an industrial research-and-development and systems-engineering management cult with unparalleled private economic and public decision-making power."

> For almost three decades the nation's resources have been commanded by military needs, and the political and economic power have been consolidated behind defense priorities. . . . The surviving myths of private enterprise insulate the industrial giants from social control, distorting the national reading of realities at home and abroad, concealing the galloping pace of corporate mergers and economic concentration, protecting the quasi-public status of narrow private interests. . . . In addition to claims of security, national prestige, and prosperity, the sacred name of science is hailed as a surrogate consensus, an alibi to soften, defer, and deflect the growing divisions of American society. . . . The science-technology race provided an avenue of substitute pump-priming which maintained personal income without increasing civilian goods, further aggravating inequities in the structure of purchasing power which commands and organizes national resources.

In his analysis of these developments, and in his passionate denunciation of their perverse and inhuman character, Nieburg is acting in the highest tradition of the critical intellectual. He is unrealistic, however, when he suggests that enlightened bureaucrats—McNamara, for example—can use the undeniable power of the federal government to ameliorate the situation in any fundamental way by working from within; just as the scientists who rightly fear a nuclear catastrophe are deluding themselves if they believe that private lectures to government bureaucrats on the irrationality of an arms or space race will succeed in changing national priorities. Similarly, it may be true, in the abstract, that "the techniques of economic stimulation and stabilization are simply neutral administrative tools capable of distributing national income either more or less equitably, improving the relative bargaining position of either unions or employers, and increasing or decreasing the importance of the public sector of the economy."[56] But in the real world, as the same author points out, these "neutral administrative tools" are applied "within the context of a consensus whose limits are defined by the business community." The tax reforms of the "new economics" benefit the rich.[57] Urban renewal, the war on poverty, expenditures for science and education, turn out, in large measure, to be a subsidy to the already privileged.

There are a number of ways in which the intellectual who is aware of these facts can hope to change them. He might, for example, try to "humanize" the meritocratic or corporate elite or the government bureaucrats closely allied to them, a plan that has seemed plausible to many scientists and social scientists. He might try to contribute to the formation of a new or revitalized reformist political party, operating within the framework of conventional politics.[58] He can try to ally himself with—to help create—a mass movement committed to far more radical social change. He can act as an individual in resistance to the demands placed on him, or the temptations offered to him, by a society that affords him privilege and affluence if he will accept the limits "defined by the business community" and the technical intelligentsia allied to it. He can try to organize large-scale resistance by the technical intelligentsia to the nightmare they are helping to create, and to find ways in which their skills can be put to a constructive social use, perhaps in cooperation with a popular movement that searches for new social forms.

The importance of collective action—obvious enough in itself—becomes still more clear when the question is approached in more general terms. In a society of isolated and competitive individuals, there are few opportunities for effective action against repressive institutions or deep-seated social forces. The point is underscored, in a different but related connection, in some pertinent remarks by Galbraith on the management of demand, which, he observes:

> is in all respects an admirably subtle arrangement in social design. It works not on the individual but on the mass. Any individual can contract out from its influence. This being so, no case for individual compulsion in the purchase of any product can be established. To all who object there is a natural answer: You are at liberty to leave! Yet there is slight danger that enough people will ever assert their individuality to impair the management of mass behavior.[59]

The real threat that has been posed by organized resistance in the past few years has been to the "management of mass behavior." There are circumstances when one can assert his own individuality only by being prepared to act collectively. He can thus overcome the social fragmentation that prevents him from coming to recognize his real interests, and can learn how to defend these interests. It is quite possible that the society will tolerate individuals who "contract out," but only insofar as they do not organize to do so collectively, thus impairing "the management of mass behavior" that is a crucial feature of a society designed along the lines that appeal to the liberal technocrats (compare the remarks by Mc-Namara cited above) or to the radical centralizers of whom the Bolshevik ideologists have been the most prominent examples.

In small but important ways, such tasks as those suggested above are being undertaken—for example, by the students and junior faculty who have formed a Committee of Concerned Asian Scholars to try to reconstruct Asian studies on a basis that is both more objective and more humane, and in this way strike at one of the underpinnings of the aggressive ideology that supports the national commitment to repression, social management on a global scale, and ultimately, destruction; or by groups of scientists and engineers who are just now beginning to organize in opposition to the demands of the military-industrial-academic complex, a development of very great potential; or by those who, recognizing that university teaching and research are, in large measure, conditioned by the demands of the privileged, are seeking to construct alternative programs of study and action, of teaching and research, that will be more compelling on intellectual and moral grounds, will change the character of the university by changing not their formal structures—a relatively insignificant matter—but what is actually done by students and faculty in the university, and will reorient the lives of those who pass through it; or, outside the university, by those who are resisting the war machine directly or who are working to create alternative social institutions that might, ultimately, serve as the cells of a very different society; or those who are trying to organize, and to learn, in communities or factories; or those who attempt to construct a political movement that will integrate such efforts on a national, in fact international, scale.

Other examples might be mentioned. I see no reason why there should be conflict between such efforts as these. We cannot know which will prove successful, or how far they can advance, or how experience may cause them to develop, or, in detail, what vision of a new society might grow out of thought and action directed to these ends. We can predict that the elitist and authoritarian tendencies to which intellectuals are all too prone will subvert such efforts unless they are vigorously combatted. We can predict that only mass participation in planning, decision-making, and reconstruction of social institutions—"the active, untrammeled, energetic political life of the broadest masses of the people"—will create the "spiritual transformation in the masses" that is a prerequisite for any advance in social evolution and that will solve the myriad problems of social reconstruction in a decent and humane fashion. We can also predict that if such efforts become effective and significant in scale, they will meet with repression and force. Whether or not they can withstand such force will be determined by the strength and cohesiveness they have developed, as part of a general, integrated movement with a strong base of popular support in many social strata, support by people whose ideals and hopes are given form by this movement and the social forms it tries to bring to reality.

It has always been taken for granted by radical thinkers, and quite rightly so, that effective political action that threatens entrenched social interests will lead to "confrontation" and repression. It is, correspond-ingly, a sign of intellectual bankruptcy for the left to seek to construct "confrontations"; it is a clear indication that the efforts to organize sig-nificant social action have failed. Impatience, horror at evident atrocities, may impel one to seek an immediate confrontation with authority. This can be extremely valuable in one of two ways: by posing a threat to the interests of those who are implementing specific policies; or by bringing to the consciousness of others a reality that is much too easy to forget. But the search for confrontations can also be a kind of self-indulgence that may abort a movement for social change and condemn it to irrele-vance and disaster. A confrontation that grows out of effective policies may be unavoidable, but one who takes his own rhetoric seriously will seek to delay a confrontation until he can hope to emerge successful, ei-ther in the narrower senses noted above or in the far more important sense of bringing about, through this success, some substantive change in institutions. Particularly objectionable is the idea of designing con-frontations so as to manipulate the unwitting participants into accepting a point of view that does not grow out of meaningful experience, out of real understanding. This is not only a testimony to political irrelevance, but also, precisely because it is manipulative and coercive, a proper tactic only for a movement that aims to maintain an elitist and authoritarian form of organization.

The opposite danger is "co-optation," again, a real problem. Even the most radical program cannot escape this danger. Consider the idea of workers' councils. Attempts at implementation have frequently led not to a radically new form of management by producers, but to adminis-tration of welfare programs or even improved factory discipline.[60] This possibility is recognized by those concerned with more efficient "indus-trial management" as a potential benefit, from their point of view, of council organization. Thus in his introduction to Sturmthal's study, John T. Dunlop, a Harvard economist who has won considerable reputation in industrial arbitration, writes:

> There is keen interest in the plant level, in the relations among the
> worker, his superior, and the labor representative, in both the ad-

vanced and the newly developing countries. Governments, managers, and labor organizations everywhere are concerned with ways of eliciting improved effort and performance; they are exploring new ways of training and supervising a workforce, and they seek new procedures to develop discipline and to settle complaints or dissipate protest. The range of experience with workers' councils provides a record of general interest to those shaping or modifying industrial relations and economic institutions.

What can be said of workers' councils is true, a fortiori, of any other attempt at radical reconstruction of existing institutions. In fact, some have even argued that Marxism as a social movement served primarily to "socialize" the proletariat and integrate it more effectively into the industrial society.[61] Those who oppose a plan merely on grounds of the possibility (even likelihood) of co-optation merely signal that they are opposed to everything imaginable.

To an unprecedented extent, the university has become the gathering place for intellectuals and technical intelligentsia, attracting not only scientists and scholars, but even writers and artists and political activists. The causes and consequences can be argued, but the fact is fairly clear. The Port Huron statement of SDS (Students for a Democratic Society) expressed the hope that the university can become "a potential base and agency in the movement for social change"; by permitting "the political life to be an adjunct to the academic one, and action to be informed by reason," it can contribute to the emergence of a genuine New Left that will be "a left with real intellectual skills, committed to deliberativeness, honesty, and reflection as working tools."[62] Many in the New Left now think of such ideas as part of their "liberal past," to be abandoned in the light of the new consciousness that has since been achieved. I disagree with this judgment. The left badly needs understanding of present society, its long-range tendencies, the possibilities for alternative forms of social organization, and a reasoned analysis of how social change can come about. Objective scholarship can contribute to this understanding. We do not know, for a fact, that the universities will not permit honest social inquiry over a broad range, scholarship that will, as many of us believe, lead to radical conclusions if conducted seriously and in an open-minded and independent way. We do not know because the attempt has barely been made. The major obstacles, so far, have been the unwillingness of students to undertake the serious work required and the general fears of the faculty that their guild structure may be threatened. It is convenient, perhaps, but mistaken to pretend that the problem, up to now at least, has been the unwillingness of trustees and administrators to tolerate such attempts. Cases of repression can be found, and they are deplorable, but they do not constitute the heart of the problem. I think that the movement has been ridden by certain fantasies on this score.

Consider, for example, the argument of one well-informed activist that the goal of university agitation should be to build "anti-imperialist struggles in which the University administration is a clear enemy."[63] This is much too easy. In fact, whatever the organization chart may seem to show, the universities—at least, the "elite" universities—are relatively decentralized institutions in which most important decisions as to teaching and research are taken by the faculty, usually at the departmental level. Only when a serious and committed attempt to create alternatives within the university has been blocked by administrative fiat (or by trustee intervention) will such judgments be appropriate. For the moment, such cases are exceptions. The great problem has been, as noted, the failure to make the attempt in a serious way. It would not be a great surprise to discover, when such an attempt is made, that it is blocked—though I would be inclined to speculate that the faculty will prove more of a barrier than trustees and administration. Here too is a case where confrontations may take place as a result of effective, principled, and meaningful action. They should not be sought, nor should they necessarily be avoided at the proper time.

To mention just one case, if the attempt to organize scientists to find meaningful alternatives to the subversion of their disciplines proves successful, it is fair to suppose that this action will become an "illegal conspiracy," precisely because it threatens "the health of the state" in the manner indicated earlier. At that point the organizers of such a movement will find themselves faced with the necessity for resistance. They will have to devise forms of action to combat such a repression, if in fact their politics threatens entrenched social forces to the extent that repression is undertaken.

The opportunities for intellectuals to take part in a genuine movement for social change are many and varied, and I think that certain general principles are clear. They must be willing to face facts and refrain from erecting convenient fantasies.[64] They must be willing to undertake the hard and serious intellectual work that is required for a real contribution to understanding. They must avoid the temptation to join a repressive elite and must help create the mass politics that will counteract—and ultimately control and replace—the strong tendencies toward centralization and authoritarianism that are deeply rooted but not inescapable. They must be prepared to face repression and to act in defense of the values they profess. In an advanced industrial society, many possibilities exist for active popular participation in the control of major institutions and the reconstruction of social life. The rule of a technocratic meritocracy, allied or subordinated to a corporate elite, does not appear inevitable, though it is not unlikely. So little is understood that no forecast can be given more than a minimal degree of credence. To some extent, we can create the future rather than merely observing the flow of events. Given the stakes, it would be criminal to let real opportunities pass unexplored.

TWO

An Exception to the Rules*

When is the resort to violence justified in international affairs? What acts are legitimate in the conduct of war? These questions raise difficult problems of ethical judgment and historical analysis. Michael Walzer insists, quite correctly, that beyond merely "describ[ing] the judgments and justifications that people commonly put forward, [we] can analyze these moral claims, seek out their coherence, lay bare the principles that they exemplify." His aim is to develop a certain conception of our "moral world," and to draw from it both specific judgments on historical events and operative criteria for resolving future dilemmas.

There are certain beliefs on these matters that are so widely held as to deserve to be called "standard." With regard to the question of resorting to violence, the standard doctrine holds that it is justified in self-defense or as a response to imminent armed attack, often construed in the words of Daniel Webster in the Caroline case, which Walzer quotes: "instant, overwhelming, leaving no choice of means, and no moment for deliberation." This part of the standard doctrine Walzer calls "the legalist paradigm." With regard to the exercise of force, another part of the standard

---

*From "An Exception to the Rules," *Inquiry*, April 17, 1978. Review of Michael Walzer, *Just and Unjust Wars* (New York: Basic Books, 1977).

doctrine constitutes what Walzer calls "the war convention," consisting of such principles as, for instance, that prisoners should not be massacred and civilians should not be the direct objects of attack.

The standard doctrine, which is codified in various international conventions, holds that both the resort to war and the means employed in warfare fall within the realm of moral discourse. There has been extensive discussion of these issues in the context of the Vietnam War, the conflict that prompted Walzer's concern. While the standard doctrine is regularly violated, it remains a worthwhile endeavor to evaluate and refine it.

Walzer argues that the legalist paradigm is too restrictive in certain respects. In other respects, however, he interprets its strictly, as he does the war convention. Walzer takes the anti-Axis effort in Europe in World War II to be "the paradigm . . . of a justified struggle"; Nazism, he believes, "lies at the outer limits of exigency, at a point where we are likely to find ourselves united in fear and abhorrence." Nevertheless, he condemns as illegitimate under the legalist paradigm Churchill's decision to mine the territorial waters of neutral Norway in order to prevent ore shipments to Nazi Germany, and he considers the terror bombing of German cities to be a serious violation of the war convention. As these examples illustrate, he construes the standard doctrine strictly, even in the extreme case of the struggle against Nazism.

Walzer points out that it is impossible within the confines of his study to present an elaborate historical argument, but to me, at least, the above conclusions seem reasonable. Furthermore, Walzer is right to challenge widely accepted views, for example with regard to terror bombing. It is enough to recall the fundamental moral flaw of the Nuremberg tribunal, graphically revealed by Telford Taylor's observation, in Nuremberg and Vietnam, that "there was no basis for criminal charges against German or Japanese" leaders for aerial bombardment because "both sides had played the terrible game of urban destruction—the Allies far more successfully." As it turns out, the operational definition of a "crime of war" is a criminal activity of which the defeated enemies, but not the victors, are guilty. The consequences of this moral stance were soon to be seen in Korea and Vietnam. It would be naive to suppose that a serious moral critique would have prevented further criminal acts of the sort condoned (or ignored) under the Nuremberg principles. Nevertheless, the example illustrates the seriousness of the enterprise in which Walzer is engaged.

Even the most profound justification of the standard doctrine would be of limited import, since it is in any case widely accepted in principle, if not in practice. Hence the major interest of Walzer's study lies in the modifications and refinements he proposes, as in his restrictive interpretation of the war convention. Since the burden of justification rests on those who employ force, the still more significant part of his study lies in those departures from the standard doctrine that advocate its relaxation. These relate to the legalist paradigm of the justified use of force.

Walzer suggests four modifications that extend the legalist paradigm. Three of these revisions "have this form: States can be invaded and wars justly begun to assist secessionist movements (once they have demonstrated their representative character), to balance the prior interventions of other powers, and to rescue peoples threatened with massacre." These extensions are discussed under the heading of "humanitarian intervention." Walzer states that "clear examples of what is called 'humanitarian intervention' are very rare. Indeed, I have not found any, but only mixed cases where the humanitarian motive is one among several." He cites the Indian invasion of Bangladesh as a possible example (the only one cited), since "it was a rescue, strictly and narrowly defined," and the Indian troops "were in and out of the country . . . quickly."

There then remains to be considered one serious proposal for relaxing the restrictions of the standard doctrine; and thus much of the significance of Walzer's study lies in this crucial case. It is the case of "preemptive strikes." Walzer accepts "the moral necessity of rejecting any attack that is merely preventive in character, that does not wait upon and respond to the willful acts of an adversary" (hence this condemnation of the mining of Norwegian waters). But he feels that the Caroline doctrine is too narrow. Preemptive strikes are justified, he proposes, when there is "a manifest intent to injure, a degree of active preparation that makes that intent a positive danger, and a general situation in which waiting, or doing anything other than fighting, greatly magnifies the risk."

A single example is offered: the Israeli preemptive strike of June 5, 1967. This, Walzer holds, is "a clear case of legitimate anticipation," the only one cited—in this review of 2,500 years of history—to illustrate the point that states may use military force even prior to the direct use of military force against them. Israel was "the victim of aggression" in 1967, Walzer claims, even though no military action had been taken against it. What is more, we can have "no doubts" about this case, as Walzer states in the following extraordinary passage:

> Often enough, despite the cunning agents, the theory is readily applied. It is worth setting down some of the cases about which we have, I think, no doubts: the German attack on Belgium in 1914, the Tilanian conquest of Ethiopia, the Japanese attack on China, the German and Italian interventions in Spain, the Russian invasion of Finland, the Nazi conquests of Czechoslovakia, Poland, Denmark, Belgium, and Holland, the Russian invasions of Hungary and Czechoslovakia, the Egyptian challenge to Israel in 1967.

The Egyptian "challenge" to Israel is thus a clear case of "aggression," on a par with the direct use of armed force in each of the other cases cited. The legalist paradigm fails, according to Walzer, because, given the Caroline doctrine, it does not condone Israel's response to this "aggression."

Note the crucial nature of this case for Walzer's argument. In a review covering 2,500 years, Egypt's 1967 challenge is the single example cited of "aggression" involving no direct resort to force; nevertheless, it is not an ambiguous example, but one that raises "no doubts." Israel's preemptive strike is the one historical example adduced to illustrate the need to modify the legalist paradigm to permit "anticipations." Furthermore, this is the only modification covering supposedly unambiguous historical examples that involves a relaxation of the standard doctrine. What Walzer is proposing here, as he notes, is a "major revision of the legalist paradigm. For it means that aggression can be made out not only in the absence of a military attack or invasion but in the (probable) absence of any immediate intention to launch such an attack or invasion." Given the burden carried by this example, a serious inquiry into the historical facts would certainly appear to be in order, but Walzer undertakes no such inquiry.

He merely asserts that Israeli anxiety "seems an almost classical example of 'just fear'—first, because Israel really was in danger . . . and second, because [Nasser's] military moves served no other, more limited goal." Israeli generals take a rather different view. The commander of the air force at the time, General Ezer Weizman, stated that he would

> accept the claim that there was no threat of destruction against the existence of the State of Israel. This does not mean, however, that one could have refrained from attacking the Egyptians, the Jordanians and the Syrians. Had we not done that, the State of Israel would have ceased to exist according to the scale, spirit and quality she now embodies. . . . We entered the Six-Day War in order to secure a position in which we can manage our lives here according to our wishes without external pressures.

The Israeli correspondent of *Le Monde*, Amnon Kapeliouk, citing corroboratory statements by General Mattityahu Peled and former Chief of Staff Haim Bar-Lev, wrote that "no serious argument has been advanced to refute the thesis of the three generals." This assessment is confirmed by American intelligence sources, who found no evidence that Egypt was planning an attack and estimated that Israel would easily win no matter who struck the first blow. The chairman of the Joint Chiefs of Staff reported to the President on May 26 that Israel could remain mobilized for two months without serious trouble. "In a military sense, then, time did not seem to be running out."[1]

General Weizman's justification for the preemptive strike bears comparison to the argument advanced by Bethmann-Hollweg, the German Chancellor, after the attack on Belgium in 1914: "France stood ready for an invasion. France could wait, we could not. A French attack on our flank on the lower Rhine might have been disastrous. Thus we were forced to ignore the rightful protests of the Government of Belgium. . . . He who is menaced as we are and is fighting for his highest possession can only consider how he is to hack his way through."

Walzer properly dismisses this justification, pointing out that nonmilitary options had not all been foreclosed and deriding the reference to Germany's "highest possession," which he takes to mean "honor and glory" (compare Weizman's "scale, spirit and quality"). "The mere augmentation of power," Walzer insists, "cannot be a warrant for war or even the beginning of warrant." No doubt one can find differences, possibly even decisive ones, between the Israeli and German attacks, or between the Israeli strike and the Russian invasion of Finland—another clear case of aggression, even though, as Walzer concedes, the defense of Leningrad from possible future German attack was at stake and Russia's invasion after Finnish refusal of territorial exchange may have saved Leningrad from encirclement when the Nazis did attack. But two points deserve mention. First, Walzer does not seriously address the relevant historical background. This is a remarkable oversight given the crucial role of the Israeli strike in his argument, and given also his insistence that the Israeli attack on the one hand, and the German and Russian attacks on the other, are all "clear cases," falling on opposite sides of the moral divide. Second, a serious analysis of the 1967 case would quickly reveal that there are indeed doubts and ambiguities, contrary to Walzer's claim.

Walzer presents only the Israeli version of events leading to the 1967 war. He ignores not only the Arab version but also the well-known analyses of commentators committed to neither side. He does not mention the Israeli attack on the Jordanian village of Es-Samu in November 1966, leaving eighteen dead: a "reprisal" after terrorist attacks allegedly originating in Syria (censured by the UN, including the United States). Nor does he discuss the exchange of fire on April 7, 1967, which "gave rise to intervention first by Israeli and then by Syrian aircraft, [then to] the appearance of Israeli planes over the outskirts of Damascus and to the shooting down of six Syrian planes" with no Israeli losses.[2]

Walzer's unqualified assertion that Nasser's moves served no more limited goal than to endanger Israel is sharply at variance with the judgment of many other observers. Yost, for instance, notes various inflammatory Israeli statements that "may well have been the spark that ignited the long accumulating tinder" and discusses the problem that Nasser faced "for his failure to stir at the time of the Es-Samu and April 7 affairs." Walzer mentions that Egypt expelled the UN Emergency Force from the Sinai and Gaza and closed the Strait of Titan to Israeli shipping. He fails to mention that Israel had never permitted UN forces on its side of the border and refused the request of the UN secretary-general to allow them to be stationed there after Egypt ordered partial evacuation of the UN forces from its territory. (Egypt did not order the UN forces out of Sharm el Sheikh.) As for the closing of the Strait of Tiran, if we apply the reasoning that Walzer feels is appropriate in the case of the German attack on Belgium, we see that there remained unexploited possibilities for peaceful settlement. For example, the matter might have been referred to the International Court of Justice, as Egypt had been requesting since 1957. This proposal was always rejected by Israel, possibly because it agreed with John Foster Dulles that "there is a certain amount of plausibility from the standpoint of international law, perhaps, to [the Arab] claims" (though the United States disagreed with this conclusion.)

It also seems that Nasser may have had some legitimate cause for concern when he heard Levi Eshkol, the Israeli Prime Minister, declare that "we shall hit when, where, and how we choose," or when he learned that the Israeli chief of intelligence, General Yariv, had informed the international press that "I think that the only sure and safe answer to the problem is a military operation of great size and strength" against Syria. Nasser alluded to these statements in his May 23 speech, in which he noted various Israeli threats against Syria. And his concern may have been augmented—quite understandably—by the memory of the surprise Israeli attack of 1956, at a time when Egypt was making serious efforts to quiet the border.

My remarks here only scratch the surface of the issue. The point is that the historical record is far more complex and ambiguous than Walzer makes it out to be. His statement that Egypt's "challenge" is a simple and indubitable case of aggression," on par with the Nazi conquests in Europe, can hardly be taken seriously. Furthermore, he ignores the aftermath of the Israeli attack. Quite unlike the case of Bangladesh, the Israeli army did not leave. Rather, it prepared for a continuing occupation, with a clearly stated policy aimed at the eventual annexation of some areas, the actual annexation of eastern Jerusalem, and a program of settlement and integration of the occupied territories—a program that continues in the face of nearly unanimous international condemnation.

Some 200,000 West Bank Arabs fled during the Israeli attack in 1967, and about the same number fled or were forcibly expelled after the cease-fire. For many months afterward, UN Chief of Staff General Odd Bull reports, "The Israelis encouraged their departure by various means, just as they had in 1948." As late as the following November, he adds, "There can certainly be no doubt that many thousands of Arabs at this time fled across the Jordan to the East Bank, even though there may be no precise evidence of the methods that were employed to ensure their departure." Thus the land was "liberated"—freed of a large part of its population. The Israelis instituted a military regime in the conquered areas that differs from others of the same type primarily in the favorable press that it has enjoyed in the United States. All of these subsequent developments seem relevant to an evaluation of the Israeli attack, as Walzer would surely see the relevance of similar developments in other cases he discusses.

I focus on this particular example because of its crucial role in the structure of Walzer's presentations of his "moral world." With this case removed, Walzer is left with no historical example of any substance to indicate that his recommended departures from the legalist paradigm are more than academic—that is, that they cover actual historical events. This is not to say that the discussion is worthless; even a purely abstract discussion of these issues is of some interest. But we no longer have "a moral argument with historical illustrations," as the book's subtitle states, at least in the crucial case of relaxing the restrictions of the standard doctrine. Rather, what we have is a mere moral assertion lacking any connection to clear historical cases.

Walzer's analysis of "peacetime reprisals" might also be taken to imply a relaxation of the standard doctrine. He argues that "reprisals are clearly sanctioned by the practice of nations, and the (moral) reason behind the practice seems as strong as ever." The moral argument he presents seems weak; it barely goes beyond assertion. His single example of a "legitimate reprisal" again involves Israel: this time, the 1968 Israeli raid on the Beirut airport in which thirteen civilian planes were destroyed in retaliation for an attack on an Israeli plane by two terrorists in Athens. In fact, the reprisal was hardly efficacious: it "aroused considerable sympathy for the Palestinians in Lebanon and brought their activities more into the open,"[3] as could have been anticipated. Walzer might have strengthened his point by drawing some of the natural conclusions of his position: for example, that it would be quite proper for Cuban commandos to destroy commercial aircraft at Washington National Airport in reprisal for the acts of terrorists organized in the United States.

Walzer also gives an example of an illegitimate Israeli reprisal, namely, the commando attack in which more than forty villagers were killed in the Jordanian village of Qibya in 1953, in response to a terrorist murder in Israel that had no known connection to this village. Walzer concludes that in this case "the killings were criminal," but the strongest judgment he allows himself is that "particular Israeli responses have indeed been questionable, for it is a hard matter to know what to do in such cases." Walzer never explains why his condemnation of terrorist acts against Israel is not similarly nuanced. For example, in March 1954, eleven Israelis were murdered on a bus in the Negev; it was the most serious Arab terrorist activity since the establishment of the state. In response, the Israeli army attacked the Jordanian village of Nahaleen (which was in no way involved), killing nine villagers. Walzer regards the Israeli retaliation as merely "questionable." But then why was not the original Arab attack also just "questionable"? Or why not also describe the Israeli commandos as "thugs and fanatics," Walzer's term for Arab terrorists (in the *New Republic* article from which this account of terrorism is drawn)? The actual perpetrators of the ambush-massacre of the people on the bus were, as was known at the time, from a Bedouin tribe that had been driven into the desert by Israeli troops. More than 7,000 of these Bedouins were expelled from 1949 to 1954, as Israel encroached on the demilitarized zones. Surely Walzer should grant that it is also a "hard matter to know what to do" when people are driven from their homes and their traditional grazing and watering grounds, and left destitute in the desert—as it is a "hard matter to know what to do" when thousands of peasants are expelled from their bulldozed villages in the same region in the past few years—actions that continue as I write, though the American press is silent.

Walzer does discuss terrorism, but his account is deeply flawed. He makes the important point that the tendency to restrict the term "terrorism" to "revolutionary violence" is "a small victory for the champions of order, among whom the uses of terror are by no means unknown." It is indeed remarkable to see how the term has been restricted in recent years so as to exclude state-organized terrorism. Walzer asserts that "contemporary terrorist campaigns are most often focused on people whose national existence has been radically devalued: the Protestants of Northern Ireland, the Jews of Israel, and so on." He then develops the following "precise historical point: that terrorism in the strict sense, the random murder of innocent people, emerged as a strategy of revolutionary struggle only in the period after World War II."

His "precise historical point," however, is precisely false, as a look at his favored example suffices to show. In just three weeks in July 1938, the Irgun Zvai Leumi, dedicated to the ideals of Menahem Begin's mentor Ze'ev Jabotinsky and later headed by Begin himself, killed seventy-six Arabs in terrorist attacks on Arab markets and other public places. There were many similar pre–World War II examples: bombs placed in Arab movie theaters, sniping at Arab quarters and trains carrying Arabs, and so on. The propagandists of the Jewish terrorist groups gloried in these triumphs. On evidence of the heroes of the Herut, the party of the current prime minister of Israel, is a man hanged by the British for firing on an Arab bus.

(And while the main paramilitary force of the Jewish community in Palestine did not systematically resort to random terror, it did not disdain it entirely. To cite one case, the same page of the official history that describes the Haganah assassination of the orthodox Jewish poet Dr. Israel Jacob de Haan in 1924 does go on to describe how the Haganah destroyed the house of an Arab near the Wailing Wall in Jerusalem in retaliation for harassment of Jewish worshippers by Arab youths; the bomb caused no injuries "because by chance the inhabitants of the house were away."[4])

Contrary to Walzer's claim, random murder of innocent people is no postwar invention of the Provisional IRA and the PLO. His point about "people whose national existence has been radically devalued" is very well taken—but it applies to Palestinian Arabs no less than to "the Jews of Israel."

The special place of Israel in Walzer's "moral world" is also revealed in his discussion of the war convention—the set of principles that apply once war is under way. He contrasts orders given at My Lai with those issued to Israeli troops entering Nablus during the June 1967 war, citing a book of conversations among Israeli soldiers. It is perhaps less obvious that he assumes that this is the most objective source of evidence concerning the humane practices of the Israeli army. But putting that question aside, he might have selected other examples from the same book, examples concerning, say, the village of Latrun, destroyed by Israeli troops, whose inhabitants were driven into exile. He might have even taken a further step and quoted the eyewitness account by the Israeli journalist Amos Kenan, describing the bulldozing of Latrun and neighboring villages under the command of officers who told their troops, "Why worry about them, they're only Arabs." He might have even quoted Kenan's prophetic conclusion: "The fields were turned to desolation before our eyes, and the children who dragged themselves along the road that day, weeping bitterly, will be the fedayeen of 19 years hence."

In another section of the book, Walzer comments briefly on the pacifist critique of the standard doctrine in an afterword, making the familiar point that nonviolent measures appeal to "the essential humanity of the enemy," in A.J. Muste's phrase, and are therefore of doubtful relevance when the appeal will not be heeded. Much pacifist theory relies on a dual psychological doctrine: nonviolence will strike a responsive chord, and violent resistance will so shape the character of those who choose it that the distinction between aggressor and resister will be erased. As Muste put it, "kindness provokes kindness" and "the problem after a war [even a just war] is with the victor. He thinks he has just proved that war and violence pay. Who will now teach him a lesson?" Walzer does not directly address these basic premises of the theory of nonviolent resistance. To me it seems that they cannot be easily dismissed, though ultimately they cannot be sustained. I've written about this elsewhere (*American Power and the New Mandarins*) and will not pursue the question any further here.

Many other difficult and important questions are raised in Walzer's study, and much of the discussion is literate and richly textured. The examples I have focused on, however, reveal a crucial moral and intellectual flaw, which undermines much of the argument. No doubt Walzer expresses a broad consensus in American society when he assigns a special status to Israel and reconstructs the "moral world" accordingly, but this simply reflects the pathology of the times. Comparable judgments on the exceptional status of Soviet Russia would not have been unusual in an earlier period. Consensus is no criterion of truth or justice.

THREE

The Divine License to Kill*

American liberal thought has, by and large, provided the doctrinal underpinnings for the construction and maintenance of the postwar international order, and the conception of democracy and freedom that has animated it, the two major themes of these essays. With their pragmatic tendencies and skepticism about overarching theory, these intellectual currents are often best understood through their application in particular cases, rather than in foundational studies, generally eschewed. But there are some exceptions. One intellectual figure particularly stands out as the source of wisdom on these matters, Reinhold Niebuhr, who was regarded with respect approaching reverence by many of those most influential in shaping the contemporary world order. For this reason alone, his thinking merits careful attention. In particular, given the concerns of these essays, it is of some interest to inquire into the source of his influence and the high regard for his intellectual contributions and moral stature. The appearance of a recent biography and collection of his essays offers a good opportunity to address these questions.[1]

Niebuhr has been described as "one of the leading intellects and social critics of the century" (David Brion Davis), "probably the most in-

*From "The Divine License to Kill," Grand Street, vol. 6, no. 2 (Winter 1987).

fluential single mind in the development of American attitudes which combine moral purpose with a sense of political reality" (McGeorge Bundy). He "is one of the saints of modern American liberalism" who "attained a revered status in the American liberal community" (Paul Roazen), "a man of formidable mental powers" (Christopher Lasch), "a towering figure among the American intellectuals and a major force in defining both theological and political liberalism" (Alan Brinkley). Hans Morgenthau is said to have considered him "the most important American political thinker since Calhoun" (Kenneth W. Thompson).

According to Arthur Schlesinger, Niebuhr was "one of the most penetrating and rewarding of twentieth-century minds," a "penetrating critic of the Social Gospel and of pragmatism" who "ended up, in a sense, the powerful reinterpreter and champion of both." His "remarkable analysis ... took what was valuable in each, rescued each by defining for each the limits of validity, and, in the end, gave the essential purposes of both new power and new vitality." He "remains the great illuminator of the dark conundrums of human nature, history and public policy." His work and his writing "helped accomplish in a single generation a revolution in the bases of American liberal political thought" with its "searching realism" that "gave new strength to American liberal democracy, or, rather, renewed sources of strength which had been too often neglected in the generations since the American revolution."

From World War II through the Kennedy years, Niebuhr was "the official establishment theologian" (Richard Rovers). He was featured in *Time, Look, Readers Digest,* and *The Saturday Evening Post,* a figure familiar to the general public, the state managers, and the intellectual community, which regarded him with great respect if not awe, as these few references indicate.

Richard Fox's well-crafted study is, as Roazen comments, "a fine biography of Niebuhr the intellectual," but the reader—at least, this reader—is left with many questions as to why his work had the impact it apparently did. Fox often does not spell out the contents of this work in much detail. As David Brion Davis puts the matter, Fox "is less successful in conveying the power and profundity of Niebuhr's best work, especially *The Nature and Destiny of Man*"; indeed, he devotes only a few pages to the actual contents of this much-acclaimed two-volume expansion of the 1939 Gifford lectures. Here, Davis alleges, Niebuhr "made a convincing case for the doctrine of original sin and suggested a way to conceive life's relation to eternity without retreating into mysticism or a belief in supernatural salvation." One therefore turns with anticipation to the text itself. But there is no convincing case here for anything; if readers are convinced, it is not by force of argument or array of fact, for these are absent.

The case that Niebuhr presents will hardly convince those who are not overly impressed with attempts "to conceive life's relation to eternity" or with the significance of Niebuhr's central theme: "The double aspect of grace, the twofold emphasis upon the obligation to fulfill the possibilities of life and upon the limitations and corruptions in all historic realizations" (*Nature and Destiny*, II, 211).[2] It may be, as Niebuhr holds, that "There is no social or moral obligation which does not invite us on the one hand to realize higher possibilities of good and does not on the other reveal the limits of the good in history."

But the secular "rationalists" (as Niebuhr sometimes terms them) to whom this message is addressed will find it banal. They will see little force in the assertion—there is no identifiable argument—that in "divine transcendence the spirit of man finds a home in which it can understand its stature of freedom" and also "the limits of its freedom," that "God's creation of, and relation to, the world . . . prove that human finiteness and involvement in flux are essentially good and not evil" (*Nature and Destiny*, I, 126–27). They will regard "human finiteness" as obvious, and human "involvement in flux" to be an equally obvious moral obligation. But they will seek no "proof" that this finiteness and engagement are "essentially good," for they are not, and will find Niebuhr's "proof" no more compelling than other *obiter dicta* presented throughout in lofty and sometimes memorable rhetoric.

It is "by the mercy and power of God," Niebuhr tells us, that "man's insignificance as a creature, involved in the process of nature and time, is lifted into significance." The "primal sin"—"original sin"—is man's "inclination to abuse his freedom, to overestimate his power and significance and become everything." "Without the presuppositions of the Christian faith the individual is either nothing or becomes everything" (*Nature and Destiny*, I, 92). Niebuhr's secular antagonist is unlikely to be surprised at the discovery of "abuse of freedom" or to have been tempted to believe that "the individual is either nothing or becomes everything," so that the appeal to Christian faith to overcome this malady will seem unwarranted at best.

Niebuhr urges that "the taint of sin upon all historical achievements does not destroy the possibility of such achievements nor the obligation to realize truth and goodness in history." This is "the paradox of grace," perhaps Niebuhr's leading idea and most influential. The paradox holds of all human activity, and "The fulfillments of meaning in history will be the more untainted in fact, if purity is not prematurely claimed for them."

The quest for truth and the struggle for justice both fall under this "paradox of grace." The quest for truth is "invariably tainted with an 'ideological' taint of interest, which makes our apprehension of truth something less than knowledge of the truth and reduces it to our truth" (*Nature and Destiny*, II, 213–14). As Niebuhr later develops the point, the social and historical sciences may find "patterns of historical development," but the attribution of causes is "hazardous not only because of the complexity of the causal chain but because human agents are themselves causes within the causal nexus." There is, furthermore, no firm ground of objectivity. History is interpreted by "selves rather than minds," and "no scientific method can compel a self to cease from engaging in whatever rationalization of interest may seem plausible to it." We must search for truth but anticipate error, and always retain a tolerance for other perceptions and conclusions. We must not "ever despair of an adequate scientific method mitigating ideological conflicts in history, but must, on the other hand, recognize the limits of its power" ("Ideology and the Scientific Method," 1953; *Nature and Destiny*, II, 220ff.).

The same holds of "the struggle for justice," which is "as profound a revelation of the possibilities and limits of historical existence as the quest for truth."

Here too, the Christian faith teaches us that "History moves towards the realization of the Kingdom [of God] but yet the judgment of God is upon every new realization," upon "the evil, which taints all (human) achievements" (*Nature and Destiny*, II, 244, 286). We must recognize both human possibilities and human finiteness. To ignore the first leads to skepticism ("in the field of culture") and to an immoral refusal of engagement (in the social world); to ignore the second leads to "fanaticism," which Niebuhr perceives in the "pretensions" of the social sciences and in the "religious faiths" of liberalism and Marxism, the thesis and antithesis that run through his work, to be overcome by the synthesis more specifically, the "synthesis of reformation and renaissance" offered by the Christian faith, the doctrines of original sin and atonement that he develops.

Niebuhr proceeds to show how these often plausible contentions about human possibilities and limits can be embedded in a version of Christian faith. Whether this intellectual apparatus is helpful in understanding the issues or fortifying the conclusions is another question. That his conclusions can *only* be grounded or comprehended in these terms is mere conceit. That he has "proven" any of this, as he often claims, is—to use his favored polemical term—"absurd."

The discussion is peppered with such words as "prove" and "consequently," suggesting that an argument has been offered. Thus we read in a critique of naturalism: "If, however, the eternity to which the individual flees is an undifferentiated realm of being, which negates all history and denies its significance, the individual is himself swallowed up in that negation, as the logic of mysticism abundantly *proves*. *Consequently* it is only in a prophetic religion, as in Christianity, that individuality can be maintained" (*Nature and Destiny*, I, 69).

The "pride and power of man, who surprises himself by the influence of his decisions upon history and the power of his actions upon nature, who discovers himself as a creator," is a "this-worldly version" of "the Christian idea of the significance of each man in the sight of God," as is "*proved* by the fact that neither the non-Christian nations nor the Catholic nations, in the culture of which Christianity was modified by classical influences, participated in any large degree in the dynamics of modern commercial-industrial civilization" (*Nature and Destiny*, I, 66). Since God's creation of and relation to the world "*prove* that human finiteness and in-

volvement in flux are essentially good and not evil," it follows that "[a] religion of revelation is *thus alone* able to do justice to both the freedom
and the finiteness of man and to understand the character of the evil in
him" (*Nature and Destiny*, I, 127, my emphasis throughout).

Whatever sense or value there may be to such pronouncements, it is
difficult to find in the exposition anything that merits such terms as
"prove" or "consequently." The citations also illustrate Niebuhr's rather casual way with history. In his intellectual biography, Richard Fox reviews
his casual way with the doctrines of his adversaries, who will barely recognize their thought in his version of it, not only in brief articles where
simplification is to be expected, but in lengthy treatises. Niebuhr is, Fox
writes, a "Christian apologist" who throughout his work begins "by erecting unacceptable alternatives to the Christian faith" but in the manner of
"the debater's ancient ploy of presenting the opposition in simplistic terms,
then rejecting their stance as simplistic." His books and papers on historical topics and contemporary affairs are also sparing in factual reference.

Evidently, many found his intellectual contributions to be highly
compelling, but this effect cannot be traced to their factual content, documentation, or enlightening selection of factual materials; or to sustained
rational argument, which is rarely to be discerned. It must lie somewhere
else. An interesting question, then, is: where? Throughout Niebuhr's
work, we find that much the same is true. Thus, he repeatedly emphasizes
that the "thesis" and "antithesis" that he combats are in reality religious
faiths, though deficient ones. "Strictly speaking," he asserts,

> there is no such thing as secularism. An explicit denial of the sacred al-
> ways contains some implied affirmation of a holy sphere. *Every explana-*
> *tion of the meaning of human existence must avail itself of some principle*
> *of explanation which cannot be explained. Every estimate of values involves*
> *some criterion of value which cannot be arrived at empirically.* Conse-
> quently the avowedly secular culture of today turns out upon close ex-
> amination to be either a pantheistic religion which identifies existence
> in its totality with holiness, or a rationalistic humanism for which human
> reason is essentially god, or a vitalistic humanism which worships some
> unique or particular vital force in the individual or the community as its
> god, that is, as the object of its unconditioned loyalty.[3]

The statements I have emphasized are plausible on a charitable reading, though typically presented without argument. Both of the spheres of human activity that he delineates—the quest for truth and the struggle for justice—rely on principles of explanation and criteria of value that are far from fully grounded in fact or reason, perhaps inevitably. Recognition of such "human finiteness" is hardly a novel insight, and does not entail any of the consequences he spells out, nor need these unexplained principles and criteria be "affirmed" as a "holy sphere." Niebuhr's Deweyite and other adversaries may regard them as either tentative, to be refined as the quest for truth and the struggle for justice proceed, or as elements of our intrinsic nature, providing a framework for our thought, action, achievement, and understanding. Such disavowal of "the sacred" leads to no new form of worship. Insofar as these ideas are reasonable, they should be considered virtual truisms, deriving from the seventeenth-century response to the skeptical crisis and the eighteenth-century Enlightenment.

"The conflict between rationalists and romanticists has become one of the most fateful issues of our day, with every possible religious and political implication," Niebuhr asserts in opening his Gifford lectures. The "rationalist," whether "idealistic" or "naturalistic," is confronted with "the protest of the romantic naturalists who interpret man as primarily vitality and who find neither a pale reason nor a mechanical nature an adequate key to man's true essence." "Modern man, in short, cannot determine whether he shall understand himself primarily from the standpoint of the uniqueness of his reason or from the standpoint of his affinity with nature; and if the latter whether it is the harmless order and peace of nature or her vitality which is the real clue to his essence. Thus some of the certainties of modern man are in contradiction with one another; and it may be questioned whether the conflict can be resolved within terms of the presuppositions with which modern culture approaches the issue."

Niebuhr goes on to assert that it is not only questionable but false, and that only his prophetic Christian faith offers the resolution of the alleged contradiction. "The fact is, that it is not possible to solve the problem of vitality and form, or fully to understand the paradox of human creativity and destructiveness within the limits of the dimension in which modern culture, whether rationalistic or romantic, views this problem. Within these limits modern culture is forced to choose between four equally untenable viewpoints": the road to fascism, liberalism, Marxism, or the despair that "contents itself with palliatives, as in Freudianism" (*Nature and Destiny*, I, 20–21, 53).

Again, Niebuhr's secular adversaries can find some meaning, and some sense, in this discussion, and the tendencies he discerns in modern thought do indeed exist. But the presuppositions of modern secular culture require no certainties and need find no contradiction between the uniqueness of human reason and the recognition that humans are part of nature. This culture will perceive problems where Niebuhr finds paradox and contradiction, and may even tentatively conclude that these problems lie in part beyond human intellectual capacity—hardly a surprising conclusion if humans are indeed part of the natural world. The appeal to Christian faith may provide spiritual sustenance to those who choose to follow Niebuhr's path, but nothing more can be claimed, and one who does not feel comforted by arbitrary faith in this or that—and Niebuhr offers nothing more—will persist in seeking truth and justice, with full recognition of the fact—indeed, the banality of the observation—that much lies beyond our grasp, and that this condition will persist for all of human history. It is all too easy to mistake obscurantism for profundity.

Niebuhr won renown not only as a thinker but also as a participant in social and political affairs, and his life was indeed one of continuous engagement, in his writings, preaching and lecturing, and other activities. Turning to his writings in these domains, we find essentially the same qualities: no rational person could be convinced since evidence is sparse and often dubious, it is difficult to detect a thread of argument, and he keeps pretty much to the surface of the issues he addresses. No serious Marxists, for example, would be impressed by the insight that "an optimism which depends upon the hope of the complete realization of our highest ideals in history is bound to suffer ultimate disillusionment," though they would be surprised to learn that "Marxianism is, in short, another form of utopianism."[4] Marx had little to say about the nature of communism and—rightly or wrongly—had only contempt for "utopianism," including attempts to sketch out the detailed nature of communist society.

In his *Reflections on the End of an Era* (1934), Niebuhr wrote that "When the storms and fevers of this era are passed, and modern civilization has achieved a social system which provides some basic justice compatible with the necessities of a technical age, the perennial problems of humanity will emerge once more." It is hard to imagine that he was not familiar with the very similar conceptions of the Deweyites and Marxists he condemns, for example, Sidney Hook, who, a year earlier, in a book expounding a Deweyite version of Marx, had written that Marx's "dialectic method" "does not sanction the naive belief that a perfect society, a perfect man, will ever be realized; but neither does it justify the opposite error that since perfection is unattainable, it is therefore immaterial what kind of men or societies exist" (a secular version of Niebuhr's later "paradox of grace").[5]

Citing Marx's words that "Granted the principle of the imperfection of man. . . . We know in advance that all human institutions are incomplete," Hook went on to observe that for Marx, as for Hegel, cultural progress consists in transferring problems to higher and more inclusive levels. But there are always problems. "History," he says, "has no other way of answering old questions than by putting new ones." Under communism man ceases to suffer as an animal and suffers as human. He therewith moves from the plane of the pitiful to the plane of the tragic. The similarity to Niebuhr's later views is clear, but neither such then-familiar work nor its antecedents prevented him from condemning Marxism and Deweyite liberalism as forms of "utopianism," to be overcome in his Christian synthesis.

Fox finds Niebuhr's "pivotal contribution to the intellectual life of the forties," when his influence approached its peak, to be "the somber assertion of built-in limits to human existence." As explained in the Gifford lectures and elsewhere, including his political writings, a person should seek truth and justice, recognizing the inevitability of the taint of interest, of evil in pursuit of good, and of the impossibility of "fulfillment" in human history. Again, the conclusions are plausible enough, though hardly note-worthy. But one will find little in Niebuhr's work of the period that would, or should, convince anyone not already persuaded on other grounds.

When Niebuhr turns to substantive political issues, the results are less than overwhelming. His highly regarded defense of democracy in *The Children of Light and the Children of Darkness* (1944) is a case in point. We may agree that "[a] free society requires some confidence in the ability of men to reach tentative and tolerable adjustments between their competing interests and to arrive at some common notions of justice which transcend all partial interests." But the inquiry into contemporary democracy, or democracy as an ideal, does not end here, and is not furthered by the broad brush strokes that follow.

Arthur Schlesinger comments (approvingly) that Niebuhr's discussion here "sounded a good deal more like the mixed economy and open society of the New Deal than like socialism." Schlesinger much exaggerates "Roosevelt's brilliant invocation of democratic resources against the perils of depression and war." It was wartime military Keynesianism, not the New Deal, that overcame the depression, and Roosevelt's steps toward war, however one judges their merits, were hardly a model of democracy—as Charles Beard pointed out in contemporary work used to discredit him completely because it struck too close to home. And neither Schlesinger nor Niebuhr confronts the serious questions that at once arise when one proceeds beyond ringing phrases in "vindication of democracy" and asks, at either an abstract or concrete level, just how democracy is supposed to reach adjustments among "competing interests" when investment decisions are in private hands, with all of the consequences that flow from this fact with regard to the parameters set for public policy, not to speak of control of the state and the ideological institutions.

Niebuhr's few historical comments in this regard are also, to say the least, surprising, for example, his conclusion that the "low standards of honesty" of "the great traditional cultures of the orient" and other non-industrial societies make democracy there unviable.[6] He seems quite unaware of the impressive record of corruption in American democracy back to the days of the Founding Fathers and beyond.[7] Fox comments that in his vague celebration of democracy, Niebuhr simply abandoned questions and insights familiar to him from his earlier years as a social activist and critic: "As the younger Niebuhr had insisted, reason was always the servant of interest in a social situation. Reason was shaped by interest in selecting some topics for attention, others for the dustbin"— to which serious questions concerning democracy were consigned as Niebuhr assumed the mantle of prophet of the establishment.

It is, incidentally, a bit more than "irony" that, just as he was writing about "tolerable adjustments," etc., business interests were gearing up for a major propaganda assault, conducted with brilliant effectiveness in subsequent years, to undermine trade unions and the limited popular engagement in politics that had begun in the 1930s, and to place public policy firmly within the business-run "conservative" agenda, very much as they had done after World War I and were to do again in response to the "crisis of democracy"—that is, the threatening steps toward democracy—of the 1960s.

Niebuhr's later work, hampered by severe physical disability, yields little further illumination. In his *Irony of American History*, we find much play with paradox, but little insight into American history. The "irony" is an incongruity between ends desired and results attained; it is "ironic" because it is not merely "fortuitous" but rather involves the responsibility of the actor, as distinct from "the tragic element" of "conscious choices of evil for the sake of good."

Throughout, Niebuhr affirms the platitudes of the period. He opens by declaring that "Everybody understands the obvious meaning of the world struggle in which we are engaged. We are defending freedom against tyranny and are trying to preserve justice" against the depredations of the Evil Empire. It was obvious then, as it is now, that reality was not quite that simple. Only a year before, Hans Morgenthau had written that our "holy crusade to extirpate the evil of Bolshevism" concealed "a campaign to outlaw morally and legally all popular movements favoring social reform and in that fashion to make the status quo impregnable to change"[8]—a status quo highly favorable to the interests of the owners and managers of American society, and their intellectual retinue. Barely a glimmer of the evolving realities appears in Niebuhr's diffuse and abstract presentation, just as there is hardly more than a hint that there was some slight taint in our historical "innocence."

We were "innocent a half century ago with the innocency of irresponsibility," he writes, and "Our culture knows little of the use and the abuse of power." The year 1902, exactly "a half century ago," was the year when the slaughter of Filipinos reached its horrendous peak, and the fate of the native population is not adequately captured in the single phrase, thirty pages later, that "The surge of our infant strength over a continent . . . was not innocent" (4–5, 35). Blacks, laborers, women, and others might also have had a word to say about "our innocence," just as the victims in "our backyard," at a further remove, had more than a little appreciation of our shrinking from "the use and the abuse of power."

In completely conventional terms, Niebuhr reviews our "Messianic dreams," which were "fortunately not corrupted by the lust of power" though "of course not free of the moral pride which creates a hazard to their realization" (71). There is nothing here about the fate of those who stood in "our" way, just as the "Messianic dreams" are not sullied by the actual thoughts of those who expressed them, for example, Woodrow Wilson, who urged that state power be used to create "the world as a market" for the trader and manufacturer: "the doors of the nations which are closed must be battered down . . . even if the sovereignty of unwilling nations be outraged in the process" (1907). At worst, for Niebuhr, such thoughts exhibit "moral pride."

Niebuhr held in 1952 that now, after centuries of relative innocence, America faced the "irresolvable contradiction" between "prosperity and virtue." "The discovery of these contradictions threatens our culture with despair." "We are therefore confronted for the first time in our life" with the question "whether there is a simple coordination between virtue and prosperity" (45–46). It is difficult to know what to make of a study of American history—let alone "the irony" of this history—in which such words can be pronounced, quite apart from the reality then unfolding as the United States devoted itself, worldwide, to the single-minded defense of "freedom" and "justice."

The United States does face "moral perils," Niebuhr continues, but they are "not those of conscious malice or the explicit lust for power"; rather, "the ironic tendency of virtues to turn into vices when too complacently relied upon" (133). This is the lesson of American history and the postwar world. The United Nations, he felt, might help tame our excesses in pursuit of virtue, "as an organ in which even the most powerful of the democratic nations must bring their policies under the scrutiny of world public opinion" (136), a stance that was comfortable enough when American power sufficed to guarantee the discipline of the international organizations. Niebuhr cannot, of course, be faulted for failing to predict the general approbation for Washington's contemptuous dismissal of international law and of the international institutions generally when they could no longer be controlled, for example, the near unanimity with which his contemporary disciples, and the intellectual community generally, approve of the refusal of the United States to agree to the demand of the International Court of Justice that it refrain from the "unlawful use of force" against Nicaragua. But a student of the irony of American history might have remarked that very much the same thing happened under Woodrow Wilson, when the United States effectively dismantled the Central American Court of Justice, which it had established, when it ruled against the United States in the matter of Nicaragua. Again, there is more than "irony" here, and this care along with much else might have raised some questions about our willingness to face a "world public opinion" that escapes the control of US power.

Throughout, his picture of the American past and present is the merest sentimentality, uninformed by fact, blind to social and historical reality. Niebuhr criticizes European opinion that "knows our semi-official ideology better than it knows our practical justice" (101). But he too consistently interprets history not on the basis of the factual or documentary record, but in terms of professed ideals. This failure mars not only his account of US history, politics, and social life, but also his portrayal of our "ruthless foe, who is ironically the more recalcitrant and ruthless because his will is informed by an impossible dream of bringing happiness to all men" (75). How Lenin and Trotsky, let alone Stalin, can be described as guided by such a dream defies understanding. In fact, Niebuhr's account of the Soviet system of tyranny and oppression is no less mystical and abstract than his discussion of American history in terms of its "dreams" and "Messianic vision" and "innocency" and "virtue"—always "ironically" tainted with the evil resulting from "human finiteness."

In fact, Niebuhr does not offer sustained argument or convincing factual discussion, but rather moral precepts. It might fairly be argued that such precepts are inevitably mundane in content, however elegant they may be in expression, and that some may find them comforting, even inspiring, a helpful guide to action and inquiry. However this may be, they fall far short of rational analysis or argument. Fox observes that his work of the early 1930s, during his quasi-Marxist phase, "gave strong support to the reigning assumption on the American left in the 1930s that the social struggle would be decided by the most persuasive propaganda, not the most compelling argument" (the "reigning assumption" quite broadly, as Harold Lasswell, for one, emphasized in his advocacy of "propaganda" at the same time). The comment holds of his work throughout.

It is commonly remarked that Niebuhr always remained a preacher. To the extent that this is true—and it very largely is—the persuasiveness of his contributions is not to be judged, or to be explained, in terms of the way he uses factual or documentary evidence, or reaches the heart of the positions of his adversaries, or provides sustained argument for his conclusions. Rather, his writings are a form of exhortation, which, at best, brings to our attention ideas and perceptions that we recognize as valid or worthwhile from our own experience, or on the basis of our own intuitive judgments, but might have missed without this stimulus to our thought; and at worst, provides rationalization for the interests he emphasized but often failed to recognize. This is not a criticism as much as a categorization; it does not question the plausibility of his conceptions and conclusions, some of which—particularly, those that are more general and abstract—seem reasonable enough, if not particularly surprising, novel, or illuminating. It does, however, still leave open the question of the source of his influence, which many commentators and associates feel to have been immense and justly so.

During a long and active life, Niebuhr took stands on many important issues. In Detroit in the 1920s, he joined the Christian left in holding
that "some kind of democratization of industry and some degree of so-
cialization of property are the ultimate goals toward which our whole
political and social life is tending." He criticized the human cost of the
industrial system and condemned "the tremendous centralization of
wealth and power in the hands of a few." He was also critical of the cyn-
icism of those "moral idealists" who profess pacifist values, in accord
with "the tendency of those who have to extol the virtue of peace and
order." On racial issues, which were of paramount importance in Detroit
as elsewhere, he took a distant stand, Fox records. By the 1930s, he un-
derwent the transition to some version of Marxian socialism that was
common among intellectuals, also adopting the fashionable view that the
role of intellectuals is to provide "necessary illusion" for the "proletarian"
because of the "stupidity of the average man."

Niebuhr's ascent to "official establishment theologian," however,
awaited his return to liberal orthodoxies, now seasoned with the doctrine
of inevitability of sin. During World War II, he wrote in the *Nation* on
"the greater measure of coercion" required during a national emergency.
He condoned infringements on "the freedom of organizations to spread
subversive propaganda" and actions "to eliminate recalcitrant and even
traitorous elements," a fairly conventional liberal position at the time.
Similarly, during World War I he had demanded "out-and-out loyalty,"
condemning even mild criticism of government censorship and holding
that "I do think that a new nation has a right to be pretty sensitive about
its unity." The United States was not, of course, under attack by a super-
power; the territorial United States had not been threatened since the
War of 1812. Those with a taste for "irony" may wish to consider the performance of latter-day Niebuhrians, neoconservative to liberal, with regard to the measures of coercion undertaken by current enemies of the
state, under far more dire circumstances, for which the irate critics share
direct responsibility.

Niebuhr was "certain" in March 1948 that "the strategic measures
which we are taking in Greece and Turkey" were "absolutely necessary";

he was referring to the murderous counterinsurgency campaign then being launched in Greece to restore the old order, including Nazi collaborators, under a fraudulent pretense of "defense" of Greece from Soviet aggression. He strongly approved of the actions of the Senate Internal Security Committee of Senators McCarran and Jenner, which were "superb"—"the Communists are really ferreted out"—in contrast to Joseph McCarthy, who vilified Niebuhr's ADA associates as well as Communists, Fox observes. In 1956, he condemned Eisenhower's critical stance toward the Israeli-French-British invasion of Egypt, which risked the loss of "strategic fortresses" such as Israel in the illusory interest of "'peace in our time." He maintained his approval of Israel's 1956 aggression, observing in June 1967 that "Now that the Israelis have given Nasser and the Arab tribes (sic) their third resounding defeat," he wished to "thank God for the little nation, which mixes historic faith with superiority in the arts of war." It is easy to see why his attitudes would generally have endeared him to postwar intellectual opinion.

In his avoidance of fact and argument, and the praise that such practice elicited, Niebuhr was enjoying the luxury afforded anyone who remains firmly within conventional orthodoxies, playing the game by the rules. More exacting standards are demanded of those who prefer not to march in parades—to their benefit, one might add. The reverential awe his words evoked reflects, in part, the shallowness and superficiality of the reigning intellectual culture, a characteristic of all times and places, perhaps. But to explain his status as "official establishment theologian" we must also attend to the lessons drawn from his exhortations.

Fox comments that the Kennedy liberals did not so much "use" Niebuhr's name as feel indebted to his perspective. He helped them maintain faith in themselves as political actors in a troubled—what he termed a sinful—world. Stakes were high, enemies were wily, responsibility meant taking risks: Niebuhr taught that moral men had to play hardball.

Here, indeed, is a useful lesson, one that Niebuhr had taught in earlier years as well. During his triumphal British visit of 1939, an "inspired limerick . . . became everyone's favorite," Fox writes: "At Swanwick, when Niebuhr had quit it/ A young man exclaimed 'I have hit it!/ Since I can-

THE DIVINE LICENSE TO KILL

not do right/ I must find out, tonight/ The right sin to commit—and commit it.'"

The inescapable "taint of sin on all historical achievements," the necessity to make "conscious choices of evil for the sake of good"—these are soothing doctrines for those preparing to "face the responsibilities of power," or in plain English, to set forth on a life of crime, to "play hardball" in their efforts to "maintain this position of disparity" between our overwhelming wealth and the poverty of others, in George Kennan's trenchant phrase as he urged in a secret document of 1948 that we put aside "idealistic slogans" and prepare "to deal in straight power concepts."

Herein lies the secret of Niebuhr's enormous influence and success.

FOUR

"Consent Without Consent": Reflections on the Theory and Practice of Democracy[*1]

The current moment is an opportune one to reflect on core issues of American democracy. The 1996 primary season is over, and the two presumed candidates are heading on to the campaign itself. As always, the primaries had extensive media coverage. There was also an unprecedented flow of funds, far more than in 1992, though only one nomination was contested. But a few things were missing, and these may be the most enlightening aspect of the primary season.

The first notable gap was voters. Apart from New Hampshire, where one-fourth of the electorate took part, participation ranged from 3 percent to 11 percent in the primaries that gave Robert Dole his victory, with about 1 million votes. The scanty voting was carried out "with great haste—and not that much deliberation," *New York Times* electoral analyst Richard Berke reported; and was skewed toward the wealthy, as usual. Whatever may have been taking place, it did not seem to be of much interest to the general population.

Also missing is much of a difference between the two presidential candidates. Both are (in effect) moderate Republicans and longtime gov-

---

*From "Consent without Consent: Reflections on the Theory and Practice of Democracy," *Cleveland State Law Review*, vol. 44, no. 4 (1996).

ernment insiders, basically candidates of the business world. A few
months after Bill Clinton took office, the lead story in the *Wall Street
Journal* reported approvingly that the President is "Wooing, And Mostly
Pleasing, Big-Business Leaders." The story is headed "Unlikely Allies,"
but that is hardly a reflection of Clinton's earlier record or campaign literature, as the news report tacitly recognized. The *Journal* was pleased
that "on issue after issue, Mr. Clinton and his administration come down
on the same side as corporate America," eliciting cheers from CEOs of
major corporations, who are delighted that "we're getting along much
better with this administration than we did with previous ones," as one
put it.

A year later, the *Journal's* enthusiasm was unabated. "The Clinton
record is surprisingly pro-business—and centrist," it reported with need-
less puzzlement. With the help of congressional Republicans, the "special
interests" have been able to "break him," gratifying the US Chamber of
Commerce, corporate lobbyists, insurance firms, and the like. Only
"some special interests have lost out" with Democrats in control of both
the Presidency and Congress: unions, who had a "very sparse two years,"
the *Washington Post* reported, while "business made out like a bandit,"
achieving virtually all of its objectives while blocking labor and progres-
sives at every turn.[2]

Aspirations rose several notches higher with the narrow electoral
victory of the Gingrich Republicans in November 1994. A year later, *Business Week* reported that "most CEOs feel that the 104th Congress repre-
sents a milestone for business: Never before have so many goodies been
showered so enthusiastically on America's entrepreneurs." The headline
reads "BACK TO THE TRENCHES"—appetites are unabated, and an
interesting wish list follows.[3] The message was sent to corporate lobbyists
in Washington, whose numbers reached 23,000 by the late '80s, up from
365 twenty-five years earlier. The number of corporate lawyers expanded
at the same rate, along with a huge increase of other programs to overcome the "crisis of democracy" that arose in the 1960s when sectors of
the population that are expected to be passive and obedient sought to
enter the public arena.

With such allies, business had little time for the Clinton variety of support. When Ron Brown died in a plane crash in April 1996, the *Wall Street Journal* reported that "corporate America lost its most tireless and unabashed advocate in the administration, one who made stumping for companies his trade-mark mission." But though he "Worked Tirelessly for U.S. Industry," the headline read, Brown "Got Little Support From Business in Return." Not surprisingly, given the alternatives then available within the political system.[4]

In 1993, however, the best that business leaders could find was someone who consistently came down on their side. And in 1996 they have to satisfy themselves with candidates located somewhere between an improvement over Reagan-Bush and even more loyal service to corporate America.

The November 1993 *Journal* report on Clinton's surprisingly good behavior was more nuanced than I just indicated. Like Democratic presidents generally, it pointed out, Clinton tends "to appeal more to big corporations than to the legions of small-business owners." The *Journal* was identifying a fault line that has run through the US political system for many years, separating more capital-intensive, high tech, internationally oriented business from other sectors—roughly, the division represented by the Business Council and Business Roundtable, on the one hand, and the US Chambers of Commerce and the National Association of Manufacturers, on the other. The latter are not "small," quite often, but are somewhat different in character. The far-reaching consensus of the business world has long set the general framework of the political system, but there are internal divisions, this being one, a matter illuminated particularly by Thomas Ferguson's important work.[5]

Returning to the 1996 primary season, money and publicity were present in abundance, but not voters or much difference in outcome. Public attitudes shed further light on the functioning of the democratic system. More than 80 percent of the public think that the government is "run for the benefit of the few and the special interests, not the people," up from about 50 percent for similarly worded questions in earlier years. Over 80 percent believe that the economic system is "inherently unfair," and that working people have too little say in what is going on in the country. More than 70 percent feel that "Business has gained too much power over too many aspects of American life" and "has benefited more than consumers from government deregulation." Two-thirds say that the "American dream" has become "harder to achieve" since the 1980s. And by what *Business Week* calls "a stunning 95%-to-5% majority," the public believes that corporations "should sometimes sacrifice some profit for the sake of making things better for their workers and communities."[6] Such figures are rarely found in polls.

Public attitudes remain stubbornly social democratic in important respects, as they have since the New Deal years.[7] On the eve of the 1994 congressional election, 60 percent of the public wanted social spending increased.[8] A year later, 80 percent held that "the federal government must protect the most vulnerable in society, especially the poor and the elderly, by guaranteeing minimum living standards and providing social benefits." Eighty to ninety percent of Americans support (and a substantial majority of these "strongly" support) federal guarantees of public assistance for those who cannot work, unemployment insurance, subsidized prescription drugs and nursing home care for the elderly, a minimum level of health care, and Social Security. Three-quarters support federally guaranteed childcare for low-income working mothers. Close to two-thirds think that proposed Republican tax cuts "will go to people who don't need it."[9] The resilience of such attitudes is particularly striking in the light of what people constantly hear, and are authoritatively told about themselves.

The consistency between public attitudes and the record of the primaries suggests some conclusions, not for the first time. But these are not the ones that have regularly been drawn, for example, by the *Journal*, which reported in 1992 that 83 percent of the public think that the rich are getting richer, the poor are getting poorer, and "the economic system is inherently unfair." The conclusion drawn was that people are angry at "their well-paid politicians" and want more power to the people, not more power to the government. That interpretation of popular discontent with the economic system reflects two essential principles that doctrinal institutions have labored to implant in the public mind. The first is that government cannot be of, by, and for the people, responsive to their interests and subject to their will and influence; rather, it is their adversary. The second principle is that private power does not exist, even though the Fortune 500 control almost two-thirds of the domestic economy and much of the international economy, with all that that entails.

In short, there is a conflict between the government, which is the enemy, and the people, who are living the American dream together: the sober working man, his loyal wife (now maybe with a job herself), the hardworking executive toiling for the benefit of all, the friendly banker eager to lend money when needed, all a model of harmony, their happy lives disrupted only by "outsiders" and "un-Americans" of various sorts— union organizers and other riffraff. That is the picture that has been diligently crafted by the Public Relations industry, vastly expanded after the shock of popular organizing in the 1930s shattered the belief that the end of history had been reached in a kind of utopia of the masters. With some variants, the picture has endured in business propaganda, the entertainment industry, and much of the popular and intellectual culture.

Given a picture of this general nature, the fact that the overwhelming majority of the population regard the *economic* system as inherently unfair can be understood to mean that people are angry at rich politicians and want the government off their backs so that "the people" will have "the power," not their enemy. The conclusion is not entirely wrong, after the propaganda onslaught of the past years, on a scale that is rarely appreciated. And the conclusion even makes some sense if we accept its tacit presuppositions: a democratic government that serves popular interests is impossible (though state governments are tolerable, being far more easily dominated by private power); and the people live in harmony, contrary to beliefs about class conflict that seemed obvious to Adam Smith and many since, and are an absolute obsession of the American business community, which is unusual in its high level of class consciousness and dedication to class warfare, quite openly expressed by business leaders. They have long warned of "the hazard facing industrialists" in "the newly realized political power of the masses," and the need to wage and win "the everlasting battle for the minds of men" and "indoctrinate citizens with the capitalist story" until "they are able to play back the story with remarkable fidelity"; and so on, in an impressive flow, accompanied by even more impressive efforts, and surely one of the central themes of modern history.[10]

It is a tribute to the skill of the warriors fighting the everlasting battle that when the dam finally broke during the 1996 primaries, there was real surprise and alarm at the appeal on class lines by a demagogue assuming a populist mantle. Pat Buchanan "opened a second front" in the "class war," New York Times commentator Jason DeParle reported. Before that, unhappy people were expressing their anger and frustration by targeting "welfare families, immigrants and beneficiaries of affirmative action." But now, they were discovering bosses, managers, investors, speculators, even class conflict, features of our harmonious society that had somehow escaped notice.[11]

Ears that were tuned to a different part of the spectrum might have made the discovery a few years earlier; say, in 1978, when UAW President Doug Fraser condemned business leaders for having "chosen to wage a one-sided class war in this country—a war against working people, the unemployed, the poor, the minorities, the very young and the very old, and even many in the middle class of our society," and having "broken and discarded the fragile, unwritten compact previously existing during a period of growth and progress."[12] Or twenty years before that, in the labor press when it still existed on a substantial scale and was seeking—in its own words—to combat the corporate offensive to "sell the American people on the virtues of big business," and to provide "antidotes for the worst poisons of the kept press," the commercial media, which have the task of damning labor at every opportunity while carefully glossing over the sins of the banking and industrial magnates who really control the nation."[13] And long before, back to the early days of the industrial revolution.

We may be entering a new "blame era," Meg Greenfield warned in Newsweek, with "a switch from a variety of other organized grievances and conflicts to a developing economic class warfare theme." There is growing "animosity towards the fat cats—the corporate executives and top-level managers and investment bankers and other movers and shakers and dealmakers in the burgeoning new business universe," where "many things are happening . . . that only the specialist can understand." Those who cannot understand are seeking "a new national heavy," someone to blame for their woes. That is unfortunate, but understandable, Greenfield explains: misguided people always look for "malign forces . . . to explain their own failures and miseries," sometimes "Catholics and Jews and immigrants," now "the movers and shakers and dealmakers" who are leading us to a new world.

"So far, most Americans have tended to blame Big Government for their economic woes," the editors of *Business Week* add, "but now their anger may be shifting in some measure toward Big Business." Many are even challenging "the role of the corporation in society." "Only the foolish would ignore the signs," and corporations must consider "the need to be more responsible corporate citizens" if they are to undercut the "reviving left." "The big reason why the bond and stock markets have enjoyed such a heady run for the past 15 years has been capital's clear subjugation of labor," John Liscio writes in *Barron's*, but the increasingly "aggressive campaign" of workers "to secure a so-called 'living wage,'" and their occasional successes in this "sudden grassroots push for a guaranteed bigger piece of the pie," can no longer be ignored.[14]

There was still greater shock and distress at the discovery that the public feels that the masters of the economy are not meeting their responsibility to workers and communities, by a margin of almost 20 to 1. The reaction merits some attention.

One should note carefully the range of options admitted into public discourse now that the harmony of the past has been disrupted by the confused and misguided public and cynical politicians. At one extreme of the broadened spectrum of responsible debate it is held that those who rule the private economy should ruthlessly seek profit, and at the other extreme, that they should be more benevolent autocrats.

Missing from the spectrum are some other conceivable possibilities, for example, the thoughts of Thomas Jefferson, who warned of the rise of a "single and splendid government of an aristocracy, founded on banking institutions, and moneyed incorporations," which would enable the few to be "riding and ruling over the plundered ploughman and beggared yeomanry," destroying democracy and restoring a form of absolutism if given free rein, as they later were, beyond his worst nightmares. Or Alexis de Tocqueville, who, like Jefferson and Adam Smith, regarded equality of condition as an important feature of a free and just society. He saw the dangers of a "permanent inequality of conditions" and an end to democracy if "the manufacturing aristocracy which is growing up under our eyes," "one of the harshest that has ever existed in the world," should escape its confines.

Or America's leading twentieth-century social philosopher, John Dewey, who held that we cannot talk seriously about democracy in a regime of private power. "Power today resides in control of the means of production, exchange, publicity, transportation and communication," he wrote. "Whoever owns them rules the life of the country," and politics is little more than the "the shadow cast on society by big business" as long as the country is ruled by 'business for private profit through private control of banking, land, industry, reinforced by command of the press, press agents and other means of publicity and propaganda." To correct this fundamental abuse of freedom and democracy, workers must be "the masters of their own industrial fate," not mere tools rented by employers, a point of view that traces back to the origins of classical liberalism. Until industry is changed "from a feudalistic to a democratic social order," based on workers' control, democratic forms may exist, but their substance will be limited.[15]

Such ideas were also current in the labor press from the early days of industrial development in the United States, as artisans, "factory girls," and other working people gave eloquent voice to their struggle against "the New Spirit of the Age: Gain Wealth, forgetting all but Self." They were struggling to defend their dignity, freedom, and culture, all under attack by the "harsh manufacturing aristocracy." They did not plead with the aristocracy to be more benevolent, but declared it to be illegitimate, denying its right to be harsh or benevolent. They were denying its right to determine what happens in the economic, social, and political realms. Like

Dewey many years later, they insisted that "they who work in the mills ought to own them," so that authentic democracy can be envisaged.[16]

All of this is "as American as apple pie," without the dubious benefit of radical intellectuals, and an important part of the authentic history of the United States. But it is all missing, even as the spectrum broadens to tolerate the thought that the Fortune 500 should act more kindly to their subjects—perhaps should be bribed by special tax concessions to restrain "corporate greed," some of the more adventurous suggest.

Apart from its intrinsic illegitimacy, benevolent autocracy poses practical problems. Those who run the game can always call it off, turning ruthless at whim. There is an illuminating history of "welfare capitalism" initiated by the masters to fend off the threat of democracy, then cancelled when it no longer became convenient, or was no longer felt to be necessary, as once again in the current era. The lessons should be no less obvious today than they were to mill-hands in Eastern Massachusetts 150 years ago.

Let us return to the primaries, and take a closer look at what was missing.

One missing item was Senator Phil Gramm, whose "well-financed campaign" was the first to die, political commentator James Perry reported in the *Wall Street Journal*.[17] Gramm's disappearance was particularly noteworthy, Perry recognized, because he was "the only presidential standard-bearer" for the "conservatives" whose "historic seizure" of power in 1994 was supposed to reshape the political landscape for a long time to come, reversing the hated social contract and restoring the glory days of the Gay '90s and Roaring '20s, when "capital's clear subjugation of labor" had been established for good, so it seemed, by methods that could not "proceed in anything remotely resembling a democracy," Thomas Ferguson observes.[18]

The collapse of the congressional Republicans is the "cruelest irony" of the campaign, Perry continued. He was right to notice these interesting facts, but they should have come as no surprise to anyone watching the polls, which have consistently shown opposition to the programs of the Gingrich Republicans.

A few days later, *Journal* political commentator Albert Hunt observed that "there barely was a mention of Newt Gingrich or the Contract with America," or other favorite themes of "Beltway economic conservatives," in the New Hampshire primary campaign.[19] True, and again no surprise. In November 1994, few voters had even heard of the Contract, and when informed of its features, considerable majorities voiced opposition. Not surprisingly, when politicians had to face the public, they dropped their agenda like a hot potato; or more accurately, dropped mention of it. That is no cruel irony, but simple realism, as is the fact that the agenda is pursued as before, whatever the public may prefer—at least as long as the "great beast," as Alexander Hamilton angrily termed the "people" admired by democrats, can be kept quiet and caged.[20]

Perhaps the most dramatic example of what was missing from the primaries was the federal debt and deficit. "Nobody talks much about balancing the budget any more," Perry reported, though it was the major issue a few weeks earlier, repeatedly forcing the government to close as the two political parties battled over whether the task should be accomplished in seven years or a bit longer. All agreed with the President, who announced: "Let's be clear; of course—of course—we need to balance the budget."[21] But the topic disappeared as soon as the public could no longer be entirely ignored. Or as the *Wall Street Journal* preferred to phrase the matter, voters "have abandoned their balanced-budget 'obsession'"—that is, their opposition to balancing the budget by large margins, when informed of the consequences, as polls regularly showed.[22]

To be accurate, parts of the public did share the "obsession" of both political parties with balancing the budget. In August 1995, the deficit was chosen as the country's most important problem by 5 percent of the population, ranking alongside of homelessness.[23] But the 5 percent who were obsessed with the budget happened to include people who matter. "American business has spoken: balance the federal budget," *Business Week* announced, reporting a poll of senior executives.[24] And when business speaks, so do the political class and the media, which informed the public that "Americans voted for a balanced budget," detailing the required cuts in social spending pursuant to the public will (and over its substantial opposition during the election and since, as polls regularly showed).[25]

Small wonder that the topic fell off the screen when politicians had to face the great beast. Or that the agenda continues to be implemented in its interesting double-edged fashion, with unpopular cuts in social spending alongside of increases in the Pentagon budget advocated by one out of six people, but with strong business support in both cases. The reasons are easily understood, particularly when we bear in mind the domestic role of the Pentagon system: to transfer public funds to advanced sectors of industry; so that Newt Gingrich's rich constituents, for example, can receive more federal subsidies than any suburban district in the country outside the federal system itself, protecting them from the rigors of the marketplace while their leader denounces the nanny state and lauds entrepreneurial values and rugged individualism.

The standard story from November 1994 has been that the Gingrich free market enthusiasts are pursuing the poll-driven Contract with America. From the beginning, it has been clear that this was untrue, and the fraud is now partially conceded. In a press conference, Frank Luntz, polling specialist of the Gingrich Republicans, explained that when he assured journalists that a majority of Americans supported each of the ten parts of the Contract, what he meant was that people liked the slogans that were used for packaging. To take one example, studies of focus groups showed that the public opposes dismantling the health system but wants to "preserve, protect and strengthen" it "for the next generation." So dismantling is packaged as "a solution that preserves and protects Medicare for seniors and that sets the stage for the baby boomers" (Gingrich). Republicans will "preserve and protect" the health system, Robert Dole added.[26]

All of this is very natural in a society that is, to an unusual degree, business-run, with huge expenditures on marketing—$1 trillion a year, one-sixth of 1992 GDP, according to a recent academic study, and mostly tax-deductible, so that people pay for the privilege of being subjected to manipulation of their attitudes and behavior.[27] These are among the many devices that have taken shape to create artificial wants, manage attitudes, and control "the public mind."

A manual of the public relations industry by one of its leading figures, Edward Bernays, opens by observing that "The conscious and intelligent manipulation of the organized habits and opinions of the masses is an important element in democratic society." "But clearly it is the intelligent minorities which need to make use of propaganda continuously and systematically," because it is only they, "a trifling fraction" of the population, "who understand the mental processes and social patterns of the masses" and are therefore in a position to "pull the wires which control the public mind." In its commitment to "open competition" that will "function with reasonable smoothness," our "society has consented to permit free competition to be organized by leadership and propaganda," a "mechanism which controls the public mind" and enables the intelligent minorities "so to mold the mind of the masses that they will throw their newly gained strength in the desired direction," thus "regimenting the public mind every bit as much as an army regiments the bodies of its soldiers."[28] This process of "engineering consent" is the very "essence of the democratic process," Bernays wrote twenty years later, shortly before he was honored for his contributions by the American Psychological Association in 1949.

A good Roosevelt liberal, Bernays had honed his skills in Woodrow Wilson's Committee on Public Information (Creel Commission), the first US state propaganda agency. "It was, of course, the astounding success of propaganda during the war that opened the eyes of the intelligent few in all departments of life to the possibilities of regimenting the public mind," Bernays explained in his PR manual on propaganda. The Commission was the official component of the campaign in which intellectuals undertook to serve as "the faithful and helpful interpreters of what seems to be one of the greatest enterprises ever undertaken by an American president" (*New Republic*), Wilson's decision to enter the European war after campaigning on the slogan of peace without victory. Their achievement, as they later put it, was to "impose their will upon a reluctant or indifferent majority," with the aid of propaganda fabrications about Hun atrocities and other such devices, serving unwittingly as instruments of the British Ministry of Information, which secretly defined its task as "to direct the thought of most of the world."

All of this is good Wilsonian doctrine. Wilson's own view was that an elite of gentlemen with "elevated ideals" is needed to preserve "stability and righteousness."[29] It is the intelligent minority of "responsible men" who must control decision-making, another veteran of the Creel Commission, Walter Lippmann, explained in his influential essays on democracy of the same years. This "specialized class" of "public men" is responsible for "the formation of a sound public opinion" as well as setting policy, and must keep at bay the "ignorant and meddlesome outsiders," who are incapable of dealing "with the substance of the problem." The public must "be put in its place": its "function" in a democracy is to be "spectators of action," not participants, acting "only by aligning itself as the partisan of someone in a position to act executively," in periodic electoral exercises.

In the entry on "propaganda" in the *Encyclopedia of the Social Sciences*, Harold Lasswell, one of the founders of modem political science, warned that the intelligent few must recognize the "ignorance and stupidity [of] . . . the masses" and not succumb to "democratic dogmatisms about men being the best judges of their own interests." The masses must be controlled for their own good; and in more democratic societies, where social managers lack the requisite force, they must turn to "a whole new technique of control," largely through propaganda.

There is, of course, a hidden premise: the "intelligent minorities" must be intelligent enough to understand where real power lies, unlike, say, Eugene Debs, languishing in jail because he failed to recognize the nobility of Wilson's great enterprise. Years earlier, Debs had been declared "an enemy of the human race" by the *New York Times*, which demanded that "the disorder his bad teachings has engendered must be squelched," as indeed it was, in what historian David Montgomery describes as "a most undemocratic America" that was "created over its workers' protests."[30]

The themes resonate to the current period, for example, when the Professor of the Science of Government at Harvard explained at the outset of the Reagan years that "you may have to sell [intervention or other military action] in such a way as to create the misimpression that it is the Soviet Union that you are fighting. That is what the United States has been doing ever since the Truman Doctrine."³¹ It is not only the resort to violence that must be "sold" to a reluctant public. Their "function" also extends to assuming the costs and risks of "free enterprise." These responsibilities of the public took new forms after World War II, when the business world recognized that advanced industry "cannot satisfactorily exist in a pure, competitive, unsubsidized, 'free enterprise' economy," and that "the government is their only possible savior" (*Fortune, Business Week*). Business leaders recognized that the needed economic stimulus could take other forms, but the Pentagon system had many advantages over social spending, with its unwelcome democratizing and redistributive effects; and it took little imagination to see that the public could be kept in line by "creating misimpressions" about the Cold War. Understanding the point well, Truman's Air Force Secretary advised that the word to use is "security," not "subsidy," when it becomes necessary to induce the ignorant and meddlesome outsiders to permit the savior to socialize costs and risks. Virtually every dynamic sector of the advanced industrial economy has relied on such measures.³²

The lessons were also understood by the Reaganites, who broke new postwar records in protectionism and sharply expanded the public subsidy to advanced industry in the standard postwar fashion. And they are surely understood today by the Heritage Foundation, Gingrich, and others who preach the merits of market discipline to seven-year-old children while increasing the Pentagon budget beyond its current Cold War levels, no longer because the Russians are on the march but because of a new threat that emerged when the former enemy became a subordinate ally, even contributing to US weapons production. The Pentagon must remain huge because of the "growing technological sophistication of Third World conflicts," the Bush administration explained to Congress a few months after the Berlin wall fell, adding that it would also be necessary to strengthen "the defense industrial base" with incentives "to invest in new facilities and equipment as well as in research and development."

Shortly after, the administration greatly expanded the flow of US arms to the Third World, thus enhancing the threat that had arisen just in time to replace John F. Kennedy's "monolithic and ruthless conspiracy."

The Clinton administration took matters a step further, determining for the first time that policy will "factor the health of U.S. weapons makers and the shape of the domestic economy into decisions on whether to approve foreign arms sales," the press reported; a natural step, now that the Soviet pretext has collapsed and it becomes necessary to face the facts more honestly.

Arms sales to undemocratic countries—a substantial component, even under the most generous interpretation of "democracy"—are opposed by 96 percent of the population. Military spending is often portrayed as a "jobs program," but the public seems unconvinced, or perhaps is not entirely unaware that the term *jobs* has come to mean *profits* in the "new techniques of control of the public mind."[33]

The problem of safeguarding "stability and righteousness" has been no less grave abroad. Consider Brazil, recognized to be the potential "Colossus of the South" from early in this century and taken over by the United States in 1945 to be turned into a "testing area for modern scientific methods of industrial development," as Washington "assumed, out of self-interest, responsibility for the welfare of the world capitalist system."[34] On a visit to Brazil in 1960, President Eisenhower assured an audience of half a million that "Our socially conscious private-enterprise system benefits all the people, owners and workers alike. . . . In freedom the Brazilian worker is happily demonstrating the joys of life under a democratic system." The United States had broken "down the old order in South America," Eisenhower's Ambassador John Cabot Moors told an audience in Rio de Janeiro a few months earlier, introducing "such revolutionary ideas as free compulsory education, equality before the law, a relatively classless society, a responsible democratic system of government, free competitive enterprise, [and] a fabulous standard of living for the masses."

But Brazilians were unappreciative of their good fortune and reacted harshly to the good news brought by their northern tutors. Latin American elites are "like children," Secretary of State John Foster Dulles informed the National Security Council, "with practically no capacity for self-government." Worse still, the United States is "hopelessly far behind

the Soviets in developing controls over the minds and emotions of unsophisticated peoples."[35] A few weeks later Dulles again expressed his
anxiety over the Communist "ability to get control of mass movements, . . . something we have no capacity to duplicate." "The poor people
are the ones they appeal to and they have always wanted to plunder the
rich."[36] Soon after, Washington had to turn to sterner measures to maintain stability and righteousness.

Responsible men who try to bring democracy to the children of the
world face no easy task, and it is therefore not surprising that Washington's "impulse to promote democracy" is generally ineffective, and often
limited to rhetoric (Thomas Carothers, surveying Washington's crusade
for democracy under Reagan, which he regards as "sincere" though
largely a failure).

The "democracy assistance projects" of the Reagan administration
(which Carothers reviews with "an insider's perspective," having served in
the Office of the Legal Adviser of the Department of State from 1985 to
1988) sought to maintain "the basic order of what, historically at least, are
quite undemocratic societies" and to avoid "populist-based change" that
might risk "upsetting established economic and political orders and heading off in a leftist direction." The United States continued "to adopt
prodemocracy policies as a means of relieving pressure for more radical
change"—much as "welfare capitalism" and democratic reforms were reluctantly accepted at home—"but inevitably sought only limited, top-down
forms of democratic change that did not risk upsetting the traditional
structures of power with which the United States has long been allied."
The word "inevitable" is too strong, but the policies are natural, expected,
and routine, and consistent with prevailing conceptions of democracy. Nor
is it particularly surprising that progress toward democracy was negatively
correlated with US influence, as Carothers indicates.[37]

Similar problems have arisen with international institutions. In its
early years, the United Nations was a reliable instrument of US policy, for
obvious reasons, and was highly admired. But decolonization brought with
it what came to be called "the tyranny of the majority," and from the 1960s,
Washington was compelled to take the lead in vetoing Security Council

resolutions (with Britain second and France a distant third), and voting alone or with a few client states against General Assembly resolutions. The United Nations fell into disfavor, and there was no little perplexity over the fact that the UN is opposing the United States (not conversely), with Washington no longer assured of "an automatic majority" (*New York Times* UN correspondent Richard Bernstein, who attributes the deterioration of international norms to "the very structure and political culture" of the UN and the lack of diplomatic skills among Americans).[38]

By the 1980s, the United States had to withdraw its acceptance of compulsory jurisdiction by the World Court for similar reasons. State Department Legal Adviser Abraham Sofaer explained that when the United States accepted such jurisdiction, most members of the UN "were aligned with the United States and shared its views regarding world order." But no longer. Now "[a] great many of these cannot be counted on to share our view of the original constitutional conception of the U.N. Charter," and "this same majority often opposes the United States on important international questions." We must therefore "reserve to ourselves the power to determine whether the Court has jurisdiction over us in a particular case," in accord with the Connally reservation of 1946, which "provides that the United States does not accept compulsory jurisdiction over any dispute involving matters essentially within the domestic jurisdiction of the United States, as determined by the United States"—in this case, the US actions against Nicaragua that were later condemned by the Court as an "unlawful use of force."[39]

A domestic analogue is noted by the President of the National Association of Criminal Defense Lawyers, Robert Fogelnest. Discussing a California initiative to allow nonunanimous jury verdicts, he quotes representatives of the California District Attorneys Association who "have decried an alleged growth in the 'lack of social consensus' and cited 'differences in the community'" as justification for this step. What has changed, Fogelnest suggests, "is that women, people of color, immigrants, gay people, political dissidents, and even lawyers now proudly serve on juries as never before."[40] On this analysis, the reasoning is much the same as with regard to international institutions and challenges to "the traditional structure of power" generally: if they do not preserve "stability and righteousness," democratic practices must yield.

At home and abroad, all of this too is "as American as apple pie." The basic point was explained cogently by sociologist Franklin Henry Giddings when the United States was liberating the Philippines at the turn of the century, also liberating several hundred thousand souls from life's sorrows and travails—or, as the press put it, "slaughtering the natives in English fashion" so that "the misguided creatures" who resist us will at least "respect our arms" and later come to recognize that we wish them "liberty" and "happiness," at least those who survive the "wholesale killing" they are forcing us to undertake.

To explain all of this in properly civilized tones, Giddings devised the concept "consent without consent": "if in later years, [the colonized] see and admit that the disputed relation was for the highest interest, it may be reasonably held that authority has been imposed with the consent of the governed," rather as when a parent prevents a child from running into a busy street.[41]

A version of this useful concept has also been adopted by the courts. Thus, denying an appeal by workers who lost jobs when Ohio plants were moved to states with cheaper labor, the Sixth Circuit Court of Appeals noted that "States and counties in the United States compete with each other for companies contemplating relocation," and labor laws neither "discourage such relocations" nor bar closing of unionized plants in favor of "a nonunion plant in another part of the country or in a foreign country," as "contemplated" by NAFTA. Furthermore, Congress and the courts

> have made the social judgment, rightly or wrongly, that our capitalistic system, Darwinian though it may be, will not discourage companies from locating on the basis of their own calculations of factors relating to efficiency and competitiveness. The rules of the marketplace govern. By so reflecting commercial interests, the institutions of government serve—according to current legal and economic theory—the long-term best interests of society as a whole. That is the basic social policy the country has opted to follow.[42]

"The country has opted to follow" no such course, unless we invoke the people's "consent without consent." And it is far from true that "the rules of the marketplace govern" or that the system is "Darwinian" (in the intended sense of "social Darwinism," which has little to do with biology)— except for working people, the poor and the weak, who are indeed subjected to the social policy established by Congress and the courts, operating under the Deweyan "shadow," and might have some thoughts on the historic dedication of "legal and economic theory" to "the long-term best interests of society as a whole."

With a proper understanding of the concept of "consent," then, we may conclude that implementation of the business agenda over the objections of the general public is "with the consent of the governed," a form of "consent without consent." And in the same sense, "society has consented" to grant to "leadership and propaganda" the authority to "mold the mind of the masses" so that they will perform their duties in our free society as do soldiers in a properly disciplined army. It is the hard and demanding task of the responsible men to present a suitable version of this to the "ignorant and meddlesome outsiders," particularly when the public is called upon to carry out its periodic task of "aligning itself as the partisan" of one or another of those who understand "the higher interest." Within the political system, that is; not in the governance of the economy, which must remain securely in the hands of virtually unaccountable power systems.

There has often been a gap between public preferences and public policy. In recent years, the gap has become substantial, as changes in the international economy have rendered superfluous the gestures of the benevolent aristocracy toward "welfare capitalism," or so it was believed until ominous signs of a "second front in the class war" were detected in early 1996.

The problem of obtaining "consent without consent" did not arise for the first time in modern America. David Hume, in his First Principles of Government, concluded that in any society, "the governors have nothing to support them but opinion. 'Tis therefore, on opinion only that government is founded; and this maxim extends to the most despotic and most military governments, as well as to the most free and most popular."

The more popular, however, require more sophisticated measures to control the public mind, as Lasswell and others have recognized, including some gestures to the principle of "consent of the governed." Frances Hutcheson had argued that this principle is not violated when rulers impose a sensible plan that is rejected by the "stupid" and "prejudiced" people, as long as there is "all rational ground of concluding, that upon a short tryal [the people] will heartily consent to it,"[43] so that they offer their "consent without consent."

The people, however, are often recalcitrant, posing repeated "crises of democracy." The problem of containing the threat of democracy had arisen a century before Hume and Hutcheson, during the first democratic upsurge, when the rabble did not want to be ruled by King or Parliament but "by countrymen like ourselves, that know our wants," their pamphlets explained, because "it will never be a good world while knights and gentlemen make us laws, that are chosen for fear and do but oppress us, and do not know the people's sores." Such ideas reappear constantly through modem history,[44] distressing the responsible men just as they did "the men of best quality" of eighteenth-century England, who were ready to grant the people rights, one explained, but within reason, and on the principle that "when we mention the people, we do not mean the confused promiscuous body of the people." A century later, John Randolph was to repeat the sentiment in almost the same words, stating: "When I mention the public, . . . I mean to include only the rational part of it. The ignorant vulgar are as unfit to judge of the modes, as they are unable to manage the reins of government."[45]

Though not unique, the American experience is surely the most interesting and most important case to study carefully if we hope to understand the world of today and tomorrow. One reason is the power and primacy of the United States. Another is its stable and longstanding democratic institutions. Furthermore, the United States is about as close to a tabula rasa as one can find. America can be "as happy as she pleases," Thomas Paine remarked in 1776: "she hath a blank sheet to write upon." The indigenous societies were largely eliminated. By comparative standards, the United States also has little residue of earlier European structures or an authentic conservative tradition, one reason, perhaps, for the relative weakness of the social contract and of support systems, which often had their roots in precapitalist institutions. And to an unusual extent, the sociopolitical order was consciously designed. In studying history, one cannot construct experiments, but the United States is as close to the "ideal case" of state capitalist democracy as can be found.

The main designer, furthermore, was not only an astute political thinker but also a very lucid one, whose views largely prevailed, and have received careful scholarly attention (with diverse conclusions).[46] While eloquently upholding the call for "preservation of the sacred fire of liberty" that he wrote into George Washington's Inaugural Address, James Madison also echoed and reshaped the concerns that have guided the thinking of the responsible men throughout the modem democratic era. In the debates on the Federal Constitution, he pointed out that "in England, at this day, if elections were open to all classes of people, the property of landed proprietors would be insecure. An agrarian law would soon take place," undermining the right to property. To ward off such injustice, "our government ought to secure the permanent interests of the country against innovation," arranging voting patterns and checks and balances so as "to protect the minority of the opulent against the majority."[47]

In Madison's "determination to protect minorities against majority infringements of their rights," Lance Banning observes, "it is absolutely clear that he was most especially concerned for propertied minorities among the people." For that reason, Madison held that "the senate ought to come from and represent the wealth of the nation," the "more capable sett of men," and that other constraints on democratic rule should be instituted. In the Madisonian Virginia Plan, the upper house was to "assure continuing protection for the rights of the minority and other public goods," Banning comments. But in practice, it is the rights of a specific minority that are to be protected, even to be considered a "public good": the propertied minority of the opulent.

Madison's commitment to the primacy of property rights, which was established in the constitutional system, is clear even in the statements adduced to show that he "differed most profoundly from some others at the meeting" by according "the people's right to rule" the same importance as "the protection of the rights of property" (Banning). To illustrate, Banning notes that throughout his life Madison kept to his maxim that "in a just and a free government the rights both of property and of persons ought to be effectually guarded." The formulation is misleading, however. There are no "rights of property," only rights to property, which are rights of persons standing alongside other rights (to freedom of speech, etc.). The right to property also differs from others in that one person's possession of property deprives another of that right. The Madisonian principle, then, holds in effect that a just and free government should guard the rights of persons generally, but must provide special and additional guarantees for the rights of one class of persons, property owners, thus protecting the minority of the opulent against the majority.

The threat of democracy took on still larger proportions because of the likely increase in "the proportion of those who will labor under all the hardships of life, and secretly sigh for a more equal distribution of its blessings," which Madison anticipated in a June 1787 speech. Perhaps influenced by Shay's rebellion, he went on to warn that "the equal laws of suffrage" might in time shift power into their hands. "No agrarian attempts have yet been made in this Country," he added, "but symptoms of a levelling spirit . . . have sufficiently appeared in a certain quarters [sic] to give warning of the future danger. The poor, in short, might turn to their historical vocation of "plundering the rich," which was later to impede US efforts in "developing controls over the minds and emotions of unsophisticated peoples."[48]

The basic problem that Madison foresaw in "framing a system which we wish to last for ages" was to ensure that the actual rulers will be the opulent minority so as "to secure the rights of property [meaning the privileged personal right to property] agst the danger from an equality of universality of suffrage, vesting complete power over property in hands without a share in it." Those "without property, or the hope of acquiring it," he reflected in 1829, "cannot be expected to sympathize sufficiently with its rights, to be safe depositories of power over them." The solution was to ensure that society be fragmented, with limited public participation in the political arena, which is to be effectively in the hands of the wealthy and their agents. Lance Banning, who among modern Madisonian scholars most strongly affirms Madison's dedication to popular rule, nevertheless agrees with Gordon Wood that "the Constitution was intrinsically an aristocratic document designed to check the democratic tendencies of the period," delivering power to a "better sort" of people and excluding "those who were not rich, well born, or prominent from exercising political power."[49]

The modern version I have already sampled, though keeping to the liberal side of the spectrum, omitting the reactionary variant labeled "conservative," with its call for strengthening "community" and "civil society"—understood narrowly, however. Participation in civil society means having a job, going to church to be encouraged to have "higher thoughts than labor agitation," as John D. Rockefeller's favorite evangelist put it a century ago,[50] and otherwise keeping busy well removed from the public arena, which is to be in the hands of the rich and powerful. The latter, furthermore, are to remain invisible, for good reasons. "The architects of power in the United States must create a force that can be felt but not seen," Samuel Huntington observed while explaining the need to delude the public about the Soviet threat: "Power remains strong when it remains in the dark; exposed to the sunlight it begins to evaporate."[51]

This account of the Madisonian roots of the prevailing concepts of democracy is unfair in an important respect. Like Adam Smith and other founders of classical liberalism, Madison was precapitalist, and hardly in sympathy with "the New Spirit of the Age: Gain Wealth, forgetting all but Self," which signaled the defeat of the revolution to working people in New England not long after his death. Madison "was—to depths that we today are barely able to imagine—an eighteenth century gentleman of honor," Banning comments. It is the "enlightened Statesman" and "benevolent philosopher" who, he hoped, are to share in the exercise of power. Ideally "pure and noble," these "men of intelligence, patriotism, property and independent circumstances" would be a "chosen body of citizens, whose wisdom may best discern the true interests of their country, and whose patriotism and love of justice will be least likely to sacrifice it to temporary or partial considerations." They would thus "refine" and "en-large" the "public views," guarding the public interest against the "mis-chiefs" of democratic majorities.

Madison soon learned differently, as the "opulent minority" pro-ceeded to use their newfound power much as Adam Smith had de-scribed, pursuing their "vile maxim": "All for ourselves, and nothing for other people." By 1792, Madison warned that the Hamiltonian develop-mental capitalist state would be a government "substituting the motive of private interest in place of public duty," leading to "a real domination of the few under an apparent liberty of the many." A few months earlier, in a letter to Jefferson, he had deplored "the daring depravity of the times," as the "stockjobbers will become the pretorian band of the gov-ernment—at once its tools and its tyrant; bribed by its largesses, and over-awing it by clamors and combinations." They will cast over society the shadow that we call "politics," as John Dewey later formulated another truism that dates back to Adam Smith.

There have been many changes in the past 200 years, but Madison's words of warning remain apt, taking new meaning with the establish-ment of huge, largely unaccountable private tyrannies—Jefferson's "bank-ing institutions and moneyed incorporations"—that were granted extraordinary powers early in this century. They mimic totalitarian forms in their internal structure, receive ample "largesses" from the states they largely dominate, and have gained substantial control over the domestic and international economy as well as the informational and doctrinal systems, bringing to mind another of Madison's concerns: that "[a] pop-ular Government, without popular information, or the means of acquir-ing it, is but a Prologue to a Farce or a Tragedy; or perhaps both."

With these realities in the not very obscure background, any discus-sion of the successes of market democracy is of limited real-world rele-vance. With regard to democracy, the point seems clear enough to most of the population, however well or poorly they may comprehend the workings of the forces that "can be felt but not seen." As for markets, this is not the place to undertake a serious analysis, but surely talk of markets and trade is misleading at best when "over 50 percent of the international trade of both the United States and Japan and 80 percent of British man-ufactured exports" are "intrafirm rather than international,"[52] guided by a very visible hand, with all sorts of devices for evading market discipline. And it is surely misleading to speak of "lean and mean times" when the business press cannot find adjectives exuberant enough to capture the "dazzling" and "stupendous" profit growth of the 1990s, and a headline in *Business Week* announces "The Problem Now: What to Do with All That Cash," as "surging profits" are "overflowing the coffers of Corporate America" and dividends are booming. Or to discuss the suffering caused across the board by "downsizing" when the Bureau of Labor Statistics es-timates that the category of "executives, managers, and administrative personnel" for US companies grew almost 30 percent from 1983 to 1993,[53] while compensation for executives skyrocketed (and easily retains its international lead, relative to labor costs)—apparently with little or no correlation to performance.[54]

Similarly, some caution seems necessary in lauding the marvels of the "emerging markets" when the leading recipient of US Foreign Direct Investment in the hemisphere (Canada aside) is Bermuda, with about one-quarter, another 20 percent going to other tax havens, much of the rest to such "economic miracles" as Mexico, which followed the dictates of the "Washington consensus" with unusual obedience, and less than glorious consequences for the overwhelming majority.[55]

In fact, the very notions of "capitalism" and "markets" seem to be disappearing from consciousness, much like the concept of democracy. A few examples may serve to illustrate.

A lead story in the *Wall Street Journal*, discussing the "fateful choices" that states are making to attract business, compares two cases: Maryland, with its "antibusiness image," and "more Republican" Vir-ginia, which is "more gung-ho about corporate growth" and more sym-pathetic to "the choices made by entrepreneurs." Why these two examples? In fact, the actual case studied is not Maryland and Virginia, but the Greater Washington region, one of the "top areas in the United States for high-tech, emerging-growth companies." The Washington suburbs did follow different business strategies: in Maryland, they relied on the "powerful economic engine" provided by federal spending in medicine, pharmaceuticals, and biotechnology, while Virginia put its faith in the traditional cash cow, the Pentagon system. With a "stroke of luck," Virginia's more conservative values turned out to have been the wiser choice: entrepreneurs banking on the "the death sciences" are doing better than those who thought "the life sciences" would provide more public funding, a senior fellow at George Mason University observes. "Virginia has emerged triumphant," the *Journal* reports, exploiting "the U.S. government's huge budgets for computer systems and networks," communications and information technology, and military procurement, thereby constructing "one of the largest concentrations in America" of high tech companies.[56]

The "choices made by entrepreneurs" reduce to which public funds will be more lucrative, much as in the "Norman Rockwell world with fiber optic computers and jet airplanes" described by its congressional representative Newt Gingrich, where conservatism "flowers" by feeding at the public trough.[57]

In *Foreign Affairs*, Dean Joseph Nye of Harvard's Kennedy School of Government and Admiral William Owens argue that US global power has been underestimated. Washington's diplomacy has an unnoticed new "ability to achieve desired outcomes in international affairs," a "force multiplier" resulting from "the attraction of American democracy and free markets"; more specifically, resulting from "Cold War investments" that enabled US industry to dominate "important communications and information processing technologies."[58] Huge subsidies extracted from the public under the guise of "security" are thus a tribute to democracy and free markets.

Boston international lawyer Larry Schwartz elaborates: "a preeminent group of free-market scholars," he writes, has concluded that Silicon Valley and Route 128 in Boston may illustrate the best way "to implement market principles in former communist economies," with their "interactive system of venture capitalists, entrepreneurs, skilled labor, universities, support service and entrepreneurial and supplier networks"—and public subsidies that are somehow missing from the picture, perhaps simply taken for granted as a crucial feature of "free enterprise."[59]

Joining those who are concerned about the "unprecedented redistribution of income toward the rich," John Cassidy, in an informative report on the tribulations of the "middle class," concludes that "this is nobody's fault; it is just how capitalism has developed." It is what "the free market has decided, in its infinite but mysterious wisdom," and "politicians will eventually have to wake up and accept the fact," abandoning the pretense that something can be done about such natural phenomena. His study mentions three corporations: McDonnell Douglas, Grumman, and Hughes Aircraft, each of them as inspiring a tribute to the infinite and mysterious wisdom of the market as Clinton's choice to illustrate his "grand vision" of the free-market future at the Seattle APEC summit (Boeing), or Gingrich's favorite (Lockheed-Martin), or the corporation "which retained its No. 1 spot as America's most valuable company" in *Business Week's* "top 1000" listing for 1995 (General Electric), to mention just a few.[60]

The United States, of course, is not alone in its conceptions of economic liberalism, even if its ideologues perhaps lead the chorus. The doubling of the gap between countries of the top and bottom quintiles from 1960 is substantially attributable to protectionist measures of the rich, the UN *Human Development Report* concluded in 1992. The practices persist through the Uruguay Round, the 1994 Report observes, concluding that "the industrial countries, by violating the principles of free trade, are costing the developing countries an estimated $50 billion a year—nearly equal to the total flow of foreign assistance"—much of it publicly subsidized export promotion.

Looking at the matter from the standpoint of leading ("core") firms rather than states, a careful recent study found that: "Virtually all of the world's largest core firms have experienced a decisive influence from government policies and/or trade barriers on their strategy and competitive position." "There has never been a 'level playing field' in international competition," the study realistically concludes, "and it is doubtful whether there ever will be one." Government intervention, which has "been the rule rather than the exception over the past two centuries, . . . has played a key role in the development and diffusion of many product and process innovations—particularly in aerospace, electronics, modern agriculture, materials technologies, energy and transportation technology," as well as telecommunications and information technologies generally, and in earlier days, textiles and steel. Quite generally, "(supra)national government policies, in particular defence programmes, have been an overwhelming force in shaping the strategies and competitiveness of the world's largest firms." In fact, "at least twenty companies in the 1993 Fortune 100 would not have survived at all as independent companies, if they had not been saved by their respective governments," by socializing losses or simple state takeover "during major restructuring periods." One is the leading employer in Gingrich's deeply conservative district, Lockheed, saved from collapse by $2 billion federal loan guarantees provided by the Nixon administration.[61]

It is important to stress that none of this is novel. Centuries ago, England was preaching the wonders of markets to India while despoiling it and massively protecting its own industry and commerce, the course followed by its former American colonies as soon as they were free to pursue an independent path, as did others who were able to make relatively independent choices. And "the men of best quality" and "responsible men" have rarely wavered from their vocation, from the earliest days of recorded history.

Nonetheless, with all the sordid continuities, an optimistic soul can—realistically I think—discern slow progress, and there is no more reason now than there has ever been to believe that we are constrained by mysterious and unknown social laws, not simply decisions made within institutions that are subject to human will.

FIVE

Simple Truths, Hard Problems: Some Thoughts on Terror, Justice, and Self-Defense*

To dispel any false expectations, I really am going to keep to very simple truths, so much so that I toyed with suggesting the title "In Praise of Platitudes," with an advance apology for the elementary character of these remarks. The only justification for proceeding along this course is that the truisms are widely rejected, in some crucial cases almost universally so. And the human consequences are serious, in particular with regard to the hard problems I have in mind. One reason why they are hard is that moral truisms are so commonly disdained by those with sufficient power to do so with impunity, because they set the rules.

We have just witnessed a dramatic example of how they set the rules. The last millennium ended, and the new one opened, with an extraordinary display of self-adulation on the part of Western intellectuals, who praised themselves and their leaders for introducing a "noble phase" of foreign policy with a "saintly glow," as they adhered to "principles and values" for the first time in history, acting from "pure altruism," following the lead of the "idealistic new world bent on ending inhumanity," joined by its loyal partner who alone comprehends the true nobility of the mission, which has now evolved even further into the "Bush messianic mission to

*Frumkes Lecture, delivered at New York University, November 15, 2004.

graft democracy onto the rest of the world"—all quoted from the elite press and intellectuals. I am not sure there is any counterpart in the none-too-glorious history of modern intellectual elites. The noblest achievement was a "normative revolution" in the 1990s, which established a "new norm in international affairs": the right of the self-designated "enlightened states" to resort to force to protect suffering people from evil monsters.[1]

As anyone familiar with history knows, the normative revolution is not at all new; it was a constant refrain of European imperialism, and the rhetorical flights of Japanese fascists, Mussolini, Hitler, Stalin and other grand figures were no less noble, and quite possibly just as sincere, so internal documents reveal. The examples given to justify the chorus of self-acclaim collapse on the slightest examination, but I would like to raise a different question, bearing on how rules are established: why was the "normative revolution" in the decade of the 1990s, not the 1970s, a far more reasonable candidate?

The decade of the 1970s opened with the Indian invasion of East Pakistan, saving probably millions of lives. It closed with Vietnam's invasion of Cambodia, ousting the Khmer Rouge just as their atrocities were peaking.

Before that, State Department intelligence, by far the most knowledgeable source, was estimating deaths in the tens or hundreds of thousands, not from "mass genocide" but from "brutal rapid change"—awful enough, but not yet approaching the predictions of high US officials in 1975 that a million people might die as a result of the earlier years of bombing and atrocities. Their effects have been discussed in the scholarly literature, but perhaps the simplest account is the orders that Henry Kissinger transmitted, in the usual manner of the obedient bureaucrat, from President Nixon to the military commanders: "A massive bombing campaign in Cambodia. Anything that flies on anything that moves."[2] It is rare for a call for war crimes to be so stark and explicit, though it is normal for it to be considered entirely insignificant among the perpetrators, as in this case; publication elicited no reaction. By the time of the Vietnamese invasion, however, the charges of genocide that had aroused mass fury from the moment of the Khmer Rouge takeover in April 1975, with a level of fabrication that would have impressed Stalin, were finally becoming plausible. So the decade of the 1970s was indeed framed by two authentic cases of military intervention that terminated awesome crimes.

Even if we were to accept the most extreme claims of the chorus of adulation for the leaders of the "enlightened states" in the 1990s, there was nothing that comes close to the humanitarian consequences of the resort to force that framed the decade of the 1970s. So why did that decade not bring about a "normative revolution" with the foreign policy of the saviors basking in a "saintly glow"? The answer is simplicity itself, but apparently can't be stated; at least, I have never seen a hint of it in the deluge of literature on this topic. The interventions of the 1970s had two fundamental flaws: (1) They were carried out by the wrong agents, *them*, not *us*; (2) Both were bitterly denounced by the leader of the enlightened states, and the perpetrators of the crime of terminating genocide were harshly punished, particularly Vietnam, subjected to a US-backed Chinese invasion to teach the criminals a lesson for bringing Pol Pot's crimes to an end, then severe sanctions, and direct US-UK support for the ousted Khmer Rouge. It follows that the 1970s could not have brought about a "normative revolution," and no one has ever suggested that it did.

The guiding principle is elementary. Norms are established by the powerful, in their own interests, and with the acclaim of responsible intellectuals. These may be close to historical universals. I have been looking for exceptions for many years. There are a few, but not many.

Sometimes the principle is explicitly recognized. The norm for post–World War II international justice was established at Nuremberg. To bring the Nazi criminals to justice, it was necessary to devise definitions of "war crime" and "crime against humanity." Telford Taylor, chief counsel for the prosecution and a distinguished international lawyer and historian, has explained candidly how this was done:

> Since both sides in World War II had played the terrible game of urban destruction—the Allies far more successfully—there was no basis for criminal charges against Germans or Japanese, and in fact no such charges were brought. . . . Aerial bombardment had been used so extensively and ruthlessly on the Allied side as well as the

Axis side that neither at Nuremberg nor Tokyo was the issue made a part of the trials.[3]

The operative definition of "crime" is: "Crime that you carried out but we did not." To underscore the fact, Nazi war criminals were absolved if the defense could show that their US counterparts carried out the same crimes.

Taylor concludes that "to punish the foe—especially the vanquished foe—for conduct in which the enforcer nation has engaged, would be so grossly inequitable as to discredit the laws themselves." That is correct, but the operative definition also discredits the laws themselves, along with all subsequent tribunals. Taylor provides this background as part of his explanation of why US bombing in Vietnam was not a war crime. His argument is plausible, further discrediting the laws themselves. Some of the subsequent tribunals are discredited in perhaps even more extreme ways, such as the Yugoslavia vs. NATO case now being adjudicated by the International Court of Justice. The US was excused, correctly, on the basis of its argument that it is not subject to the jurisdiction of the Court in this case. The reason is that the US signed the Genocide Convention (which is at issue here) with a reservation stating that it is inapplicable to the United States.

In an outraged comment on the efforts of Justice Department lawyers to demonstrate that the president has the right to authorize torture, Yale Law School Dean Howard Koh—who, as Assistant Secretary of State, had presented Washington's denunciation of all forms of torture to the international community—said, "The notion that the president has the constitutional power to permit torture is like saying he has the constitutional power to commit genocide."[4] The same legal advisers should have little difficulty arguing that the president does indeed have that right.

The Nuremberg Tribunal is commonly described by distinguished figures in the field of international law and justice as "the birth of universal jurisdiction."[5] That is correct only if we understand "universality" in accord with the practice of the enlightened states, which defines "universal" as "applicable to others only," particularly enemies. The proper conclusion, at Nuremberg and since, would have been to punish the victors as well as the vanquished foe. Neither at the postwar trials nor subsequently have the powerful been subjected to the rules, not because they have not carried out crimes—of course they have—but because they are immune under prevailing standards of morality. The victims appear to understand well enough. Wire services report from Iraq that "If Iraqis ever see Saddam Hussein in the dock, they want his former American allies shackled beside him."[6] That inconceivable event would be a radical revision of the fundamental principle of international justice: tribunals must be restricted to the crimes of others.

There is a marginal exception, which in fact underscores the force of the rule. Punishment is permissible when it is a mere tap on the wrist, evading the real crimes, or when blame can be restricted to minor figures, particularly when they are *not like us*. It was, for example, considered proper to punish the soldiers who carried out the My Lai massacre, half-educated, half-crazed GI's in the field, not knowing who was going to shoot at them next. But it was inconceivable that punishment could reach as far as those who planned and implemented Operation Wheeler Wallawa, a mass murder operation to which My Lai was a very minor footnote.[7] The gentlemen in the air-conditioned offices are like us, therefore immune by definition. We are witnessing similar examples right now in Iraq.

We might return in this connection to Kissinger's transmission of Nixon's orders on bombing Cambodia. In comparison, the widely reported admission by Serbia of involvement in the Srebrenica massacre does not merit much attention. The prosecutors at the Milošević Tribunal face difficulties in proving the crime of genocide because no document has been discovered in which the accused directly orders such a crime, even lesser ones. The same problem has been faced by Holocaust scholars, who of course have no doubt of Hitler's responsibility, but lack conclusive direct documentation. Suppose, however, that someone were to unearth a document in which Milošević orders the Serbian air force to reduce Bosnia or Kosovo to rubble, with the words "Anything that flies on anything that moves." The prosecutors would be overjoyed, the trial would end, and Milošević would be sent off to many successive life sentences for the crime of genocide—a death sentence, if it followed US conventions. One would, in fact, be hard put to find such an explicit order to carry out genocide—as the term is currently employed with regard to crimes of enemies—anywhere in the historical record. In this case, after casual mention in the world's leading newspaper, there was no detectable interest, even though the horrendous consequences are well known. And rightly, if we adopt, tacitly, the overriding principle that we cannot—by definition—carry out crimes or have any responsibility for them.

One moral truism that should be uncontroversial is the principle of universality: we should apply to ourselves the same standards we apply to others—in fact, more stringent ones. This should be uncontroversial for everyone, but particularly so for the world's most important citizens, the leaders of the enlightened states, who declare themselves to be devout Christians, devoted to the Gospels, hence surely familiar with its famous condemnation of the Hypocrite. Their devotion to the commandments of the Lord is not in question. George Bush reportedly proclaims that "God told me to strike at al Qaida and I struck them, and then He instructed me to strike at Saddam, which I did," and "now I am determined to solve the problem of the Middle East,"[8] also at the command of the Lord of Hosts, the War God, whom we are instructed by the Holy Book to worship above all other Gods. And as I mentioned, the elite press dutifully refers to his "messianic mission" to solve the problem of the Middle East, in fact the world, following our "responsibility to history to rid the world of evil," in the president's words, the core principle of the "vision" that Bush shares with Osama bin Laden, both plagiarizing ancient epics and children's fairy tales.

I am not sufficiently familiar with the sayings of Tony Blair to know how closely he approaches this ideal—which is quite familiar in Anglo-American history. The early English colonists in North America were following the word of the Lord as they slaughtered the Amalekites in the "New Israel" that they were liberating from the native blight. Those who followed them, also Bible-waving God-fearing Christians, did their religious duty by conquering and possessing the promised land, ridding it of millions of Canaanites, and proceeding to war against the Papists in

Florida, Mexico, and California. Throughout they were defending them-selves from the "merciless Indian savages"—unleashed against them by George III, as the Declaration of Independence proclaims—at other times from the "runaway niggers and lawless Indians" who were attacking innocent Americans according to John Quincy Adams in one of the most celebrated State Papers in American history, written to justify Andrew Jackson's conquest of Florida in 1818, and the opening of the murderous Seminole wars. The event was of some significance for other reasons: it was the first executive war in violation of the constitutional requirement that only Congress can declare war, by now so fully the norm that it is scarcely noted—norms being established in the conventional way.

In his later years, long after his own grisly contributions were past, Adams did deplore the fate of "that hapless race of native Americans who we are exterminating with such merciless and perfidious cruelty." This is "among the heinous sins of this nation, for which I believe God will one day bring [it] to judgement," Adams believed. The first US Secretary of War had warned many years earlier that "a future historian may mark the causes of this destruction of the human race in sable colors." But they were wrong. God and the historians are slow in fulfilling this task.

Unlike Bush and Blair, I cannot speak for God, but historians speak to us in mortal tongues. In a typical example, two months ago one of the most distinguished American historians referred in passing to "the elim-ination of hundreds of thousands of native people" in the conquest of the national territory—off by a factor of ten, apart from the interesting choice of words. The reaction was null; it would be somewhat different if we were to read a casual comment in Germany's leading newspaper that hundreds of thousands of Jews were eliminated during World War II. There is also no reaction when a highly regarded diplomatic historian explains in a stan-dard work that after their liberation from English rule, the colonists "con-centrated on the task of felling trees and Indians and of rounding out their natural boundaries."[9] It is all too easy to multiply examples in scholarship, media, school texts, cinema, and elsewhere. Sports teams use victims of genocide as mascots, usually with caricatures. Weapons of destruction are casually given similar names: Apache, Blackhawk, Comanche helicopters;

Tomahawk missiles; and so on. How would we react if the Luftwaffe named its lethal weapons "Jew" and "Gypsy"?

The British record is much the same. Britain pursued its divine mission in the evangelization of Africa, while exercising in India "a trusteeship mysteriously placed in their hands by Providence," easy to comprehend in a country "where God and Mammon seemed made for each other."[10] Figures of the highest moral integrity and intelligence gave a secular version of the creed, strikingly John Stuart Mill in his extraordinary apologetics for British crimes, written just as they peaked in India and China, in an essay now taken to be a classic of the literature of "humanitarian intervention." It is only fair to note that there were different voices. Richard Cobden denounced Britain's crimes in India and expressed his hope that the "national conscience, which has before averted from England, by timely atonement and reparation, the punishment due for imperial crimes, will be roused ere it be too late from its lethargy, and put an end to the deeds of violence and injustice which have marked every step of our progress in India"—echoing Adam Smith, who had bitterly condemned "the savage injustice of the Europeans," particularly the British in India. Cobden hoped in vain. It is hardly much of a relief to recognize that their continental counterparts were even worse, in deed, denial, and self-adulation.

While quoting Cobden we might recall another of his maxims, highly pertinent today, and also qualifying as a moral truism: "no man had a right to lend money if he knows it to be applied to the cutting of throats"[11]—or, a fortiori, to sell the knives. It does not take an extensive research project to draw the appropriate conclusions with regard to the regular practice of the leading enlightened states.

The common response of the intellectual culture, some memorable exceptions aside, is entirely natural if we abandon the most elementary of moral truisms, and declare ourselves to be uniquely exempt from the principle of universality. And so we do, constantly. Every day brings new illustrations. The US Senate has just lent its consent to the appointment of John Negroponte as Ambassador to Iraq, heading the world's largest diplomatic mission, with the task of handing over sovereignty to Iraqis to fulfill Bush's "messianic vision" to bring democracy to the Middle East and the world, so we are solemnly informed. The appointment bears directly on the principle of universality, but before turning to that, we might raise some questions about other truisms, regarding evidence and conclusions.

That the goal of the Iraq invasion is to fulfill the president's messianic vision is simply presupposed in news reporting and commentary, even among critics, who warn that the "noble" and "generous" vision may be beyond our reach. As the London *Economist* posed the problem a few weeks ago, "America's mission" of turning Iraq into "an inspiring example [of democracy] to its neighbors" is facing obstacles.[12] With considerable search, I have not been able to find exceptions in the US media, or with much less search, elsewhere, apart from the usual margins.

One might inquire into the basis for the apparently near-universal acceptance of this doctrine in Western intellectual commentary. Examination will quickly reveal that it is based on two principles. First, our leaders have proclaimed it, so it must be true, a principle familiar in North Korea and other stellar models. Second, we must suppress the fact that by proclaiming the doctrine after other pretexts have collapsed, our leaders are also declaring that they are among the most accomplished liars in history, since in leading their countries to war they proclaimed with comparable passion that the "sole question" is whether Saddam had disarmed. But now we must believe them.

Also obligatory is the dispatch deep into the memory hole of the ample record of professed noble efforts to bring democracy, justice, and freedom to the benighted. It is, again, the merest truism that pronouncements of virtuous intent by leaders carry no information, even in the technical sense: they are completely predictable, including the worst monsters. But this truism also fades when it confronts the overriding need to reject the principle of universality.

The doctrine presupposed by Western commentary is accepted by some Iraqis too: one percent agreed that the goal of the invasion is to bring democracy to Iraq according to US-run polls in Baghdad last October—long before the atrocities in April and the revelations of torture. Another five percent felt that the goal is to help Iraqis. Most of the rest took for granted that the goal is to gain control of Iraq's resources and use Iraq as a base for reorganizing the Middle East in US interests[13]—a thought virtually inexpressible in enlightened Western commentary, or dismissed with horror as "anti-Americanism," "conspiracy theory," "radical and extremist," or some other intellectual equivalent of four-letter words among the vulgar.

In brief, Iraqis appear to take for granted that what is unfolding is a scenario familiar from the days of Britain's creation of modern Iraq, accompanied by the predictable and therefore uninformative professions of virtuous intent, but also by secret internal documents in which Lord Curzon and the Foreign Office developed the plans to establish an "Arab facade" that Britain would rule behind various "constitutional fictions." The contemporary version is provided by a senior British official quoted in the *Daily Telegraph*: "The Iraqi government will be fully sovereign, but in practice it will not exercise all its sovereign functions."[14]

Let us return to Negroponte and the principle of universality. As his appointment reached Congress, the *Wall Street Journal* praised him as a "Modern Proconsul," who learned his trade in Honduras in the 1980s, during the Reaganite phase of the current incumbents in Washington. The veteran *Journal* correspondent Carla Anne Robbins reminds us that in Honduras he was known as "the proconsul," as he presided over the second largest embassy in Latin America, with the largest CIA station in the world—perhaps to transfer full sovereignty to this centerpiece of world power.[15]

Robbins observes that Negroponte has been criticized by human rights activists for "covering up abuses by the Honduran military"—a euphemism for large-scale state terror—"to ensure the flow of US aid" to this vital country, which was "the base for Washington's covert war against Nicaragua." The main task of proconsul Negroponte was to supervise the bases in which the terrorist mercenary army was armed, trained, and sent to do its work, including its mission of attacking undefended civilian targets, so the US military command informed Congress.

The policy of attacking such "soft targets" while avoiding the Nicaraguan army was confirmed by the State Department and defended by leading American liberal intellectuals, notably *New Republic* editor Michael Kinsley, who was the designated spokesman for the left in television commentary. He chastised Human Rights Watch for its sentimentality in condemning US international terrorism and failing to understand that it must be evaluated by "pragmatic criteria." A "sensible policy," he urged, should "meet the test of cost-benefit analysis," an analysis of "the amount of blood and misery that will be poured in, and the likelihood that democracy will emerge at the other end"—"democracy" as US elites determine, their unquestionable right. Of course, the principle of universality does not apply: others are not authorized to carry out large-scale international terrorist operations if their goals are likely to be achieved.

In this case the experiment was a grand success, and is indeed highly praised. Nicaragua was reduced to the second-poorest country in the hemisphere, with 60 percent of children under two afflicted with anemia from severe malnutrition and probable permanent brain damage,[16] after the country suffered casualties during the terrorist war that in per capita terms would be comparable to 2.5 million dead in the US—a death toll "significantly higher than the number of US persons killed in the US Civil War and all the wars of the twentieth century combined," in the words of Thomas Carothers, the leading historian of the democratization of Latin America, who writes from the standpoint of an insider as well as a scholar, having served in Reagan's State Department in the programs of "democracy enhancement." Describing himself as a "neo-Reaganite," he regards these programs as "sincere," though a "failure," because the US would tolerate only "top-down forms of democracy" controlled by traditional elites with firm ties to the US. This is a familiar refrain in the history of pursuit of visions of democracy, which Iraqis apparently comprehend, even if we choose not to. It is worth stressing the word "choose," because there is no shortage of evidence.

Negroponte's primary task as proconsul in Honduras was to supervise the international terrorist atrocities for which the US was condemned by the World Court in a judgment that reached well beyond Nicaragua's narrow case, shaped by its Harvard legal team to avoid factual debate, since the facts were conceded. The Court ordered Washington to terminate the crimes and pay substantial reparations—all ignored on the official grounds that other nations do not agree with us, so we must "reserve to ourselves the power to determine" how we will act and which matters fall "essentially within the domestic jurisdiction of the United States, as determined by the United States," in this case the actions that the Court condemned as the "unlawful use of force" against Nicaragua; in lay terms, international terrorism. All consigned to the ashcan of history by the educated classes in the usual manner of unwanted truths, along with the two supporting Security Council resolutions vetoed by the US, with Britain loyally abstaining. The international terrorist campaign received passing mention during Negroponte's confirmation hearings, but is considered of no particular significance, thanks to the exemption of our glorious selves from the principle of universality.

On the wall of my office at MIT, I have a painting given to me by a Jesuit priest, depicting the Angel of Death standing over the figure of Salvadoran Archbishop Romero, whose assassination in 1980 opened that grim decade of international state terrorist atrocities, and right before him the six leading Latin American intellectuals, Jesuit priests, whose brains were blown out in 1989, bringing the decade to an end. The Jesuit intellectuals, along with their housekeeper and her daughter, were murdered by an elite battalion armed and trained by the current incumbents in Washington and their mentors. It had already compiled a bloody record of massacres in the US-run international terrorist campaign that Romero's successor described as a "war of extermination and genocide against a defenseless civilian population." Romero had been killed by much the same hands, a few days after he pleaded with President Carter not to provide the junta with military aid, which "will surely increase injustice here and sharpen the repression that has been unleashed against the people's organizations fighting to defend their most fundamental human rights." The repression continued with US aid after his assassination, and the current incumbents carried it forward to a "war of extermination and genocide."

I keep the painting there to remind myself daily of the real world, but it has turned out to serve another instructive purpose. Many visitors pass through the office. Those from Latin America almost unfailingly recognize it. Those from north of the Rio Grande virtually never do. From Europe, recognition is perhaps 10 percent. We may consider another useful thought experiment. Suppose that in Czechoslovakia in the 1980s, security forces armed and trained by the Kremlin had assassinated an Archbishop who was known as "the voice of the voiceless," then proceeded to massacre tens of thousands of people, consummating the decade with the brutal murder of Vaclav Havel and half a dozen other leading Czech intellectuals. Would we know about it? Perhaps not, because the Western reaction might have gone as far as nuclear war, so there would be no one left to know. The distinguishing criterion is, once again, crystal clear. The crimes of enemies take place; our own do not, by virtue of our exemption from the most elementary of moral truisms.

The murdered Jesuits were, in fact, doubly assassinated: brutally killed, and unknown in the enlightened states, a particularly cruel fate for intellectuals. In the West, only specialists or activists even know their names, let alone have any idea of what they wrote. Their fate is quite unlike that of dissident intellectuals in the domains of official enemies, who are well-known, widely published and read, and highly honored for their courageous resistance to repression—which was indeed harsh, though it did not begin to compare with what was endured by their counterparts under Western rule in the same years. Again, the differential treatment makes good sense, given our principled exemption from moral truisms.

Let us move on to some hard problems. Perhaps none is more prominent today than "the evil scourge of terrorism," particularly state-backed international terrorism, a "plague spread by depraved opponents of civilization itself" in a "return to barbarism in the modern age." So the plague was described when the "war on terror" was declared—not in September 2001 when it was *redeclared*, but twenty years earlier, by the same people and their mentors. Their "war on terror" instantly turned into a murderous terrorist war, with horrifying consequences in Central America, the Middle East, southern Africa, and elsewhere, but that is only history, not the history crafted by its custodians in the enlightened states. In more useful accepted history, the 1980s are described by scholarship as the decade of

"state terrorism," of "persistent state involvement, or 'sponsorship,' of terrorism, especially by Libya and Iran." The US merely responded with "a
'proactive' stance toward terrorism,"[17] and the same was true of its allies:
Israel, South Africa, the clandestine terror network assembled by the Reaganites, and others. I will put to the side the radical Islamists organized
and trained for the cause—not to defend Afghanistan, which would have
been a legitimate goal, but to bloody the official enemy, probably prolong-
ing the Afghan war and leaving the country in ruins, soon to become much
worse as Western clients took over, with subsequent consequences that we
need not mention. Gone from acceptable history are millions of victims
of the real "war on terror" of the 1980s, and those seeking to survive in
what is left of their devastated lands. Also out of history is the residual
"culture of terror," which "domesticates the aspirations of the majority," to
quote the survivors of the Jesuit intellectual community in El Salvador, in
a conference surveying the actual but unacceptable history.

Terrorism poses a number of hard problems. First and foremost, of
course, the phenomenon itself, which really is threatening, even keeping
to the subpart that passes through the doctrinal filters: *their* terrorism
against *us*. It is only a matter of time before terror and WMD are united,
perhaps with horrendous consequences, as has been discussed in the specialist literature long before the September 11 atrocities. But apart from
the phenomenon, there is the problem of definition of "terror." That too
is taken to be a hard problem, the subject of scholarly literature and international conferences. At first glance, it might seem odd that it is regarded as a hard problem. There are what seem to be satisfactory
definitions—not perfect, but at least as good as others regarded as un-
problematic: for example, the official definitions in the US Code and
Army Manuals in the early 1980s when the "war on terror" was launched,
or the quite similar official formulation of the British government, which
defines "terrorism" as "the use, or threat, of action which is violent, dam-
aging or disrupting, and is intended to influence the government or in-
timidate the public and is for the purpose of advancing a political,
religious, or ideological cause." These are the definitions that I have been
using in writing about terrorism for the past twenty years, ever since the

Reagan administration declared that the war on terror would be a prime focus of its foreign policy, replacing human rights, the proclaimed "soul of our foreign policy" before.[18]

On closer look, however, the problem becomes clear, and it is indeed hard. The official definitions are unusable, because of their immediate consequences. One difficulty is that the definition of terrorism is virtually the same as the definition of the official policy of the US, and other states, called "counterterrorism" or "low-intensity warfare" or some other euphemism. That again is close to a historical universal, to my knowledge. Japanese imperialists in Manchuria and North China, for example, were not aggressors or terrorists, but were protecting the population and the legitimate governments from the terrorism of "Chinese bandits." To undertake this noble task, they were compelled, reluctantly, to resort to "counterterror," with the goal of establishing an "earthly paradise" in which the people of Asia could live in peace and harmony under the enlightened guidance of Japan. The same is true of just about every other case I have investigated. But now we do face a hard problem: it will not do to say that the enlightened states are officially committed to terrorism. And it takes little effort to demonstrate that the US engages in large-scale international terrorism according to its own definition of the term, quite uncontroversially in a number of crucial cases.

There are related problems. Some arose when the UN General Assembly, in response to Reaganite pressures, passed its strongest condemnation of terrorism in December 1987, with a call on all states to destroy the plague of the modern age. The resolution passed 153 to 2, with only Honduras abstaining. The two states that opposed the resolution explained their reasons in the UN debate. They objected to a passage recognizing "the right to self-determination, freedom, and independence, as derived from the Charter of the United Nations, of people forcibly deprived of that right, . . . particularly peoples under colonial and racist regimes and foreign occupation." The term "colonial and racist regimes" was understood to refer to South Africa, a US ally, resisting the attacks of Nelson Mandela's ANC, one of the world's "more notorious terrorist groups," as Washington determined at the same time. And "foreign occupation" was understood to refer to Washington's Israeli client. So, not surprisingly, the US and Israel voted against the resolution, which was thereby effectively vetoed—in fact, subjected to the usual double veto: inapplicable, and vetoed from reporting and history as well, though it was the strongest and most important UN resolution on terrorism.

There is, then, a hard problem of defining "terrorism," rather like the problem of defining "war crime." How can we define it in such a way as to violate the principle of universality, exempting ourselves but applying to selected enemies? And these have to be selected with some precision. The US has had an official list of states sponsoring terrorism ever since the Reagan years. In all these years, only one state has been removed from the list: Iraq, in order to permit the US to join the UK and others in providing badly needed aid for Saddam Hussein, continuing without concern after he carried out his most horrifying crimes.

There has also been one near-example. Clinton offered to remove Syria from the list if it agreed to peace terms offered by the US and Israel. When Syria insisted on recovering the territory that Israel conquered in 1967, it remained on the list of states sponsoring terrorism, and continues to be on the list despite the acknowledgment by Washington that Syria has not been implicated in sponsoring terror for many years and has been highly cooperative in providing important intelligence to the US on al-Qaeda and other radical Islamist groups. As a reward for Syria's cooperation in the "war on terror," last December Congress passed legislation calling for even stricter sanctions against Syria, near unanimously (the Syria Accountability Act). The legislation was recently implemented by the president, thus depriving the US of a major source of information about radical Islamist terrorism in order to achieve the higher goal of establishing in Syria a regime that will accept US-Israeli demands—not an unusual pattern, though commentators continually find it surprising no matter how strong the evidence and regular the pattern, and no matter how rational the choices in terms of clear and understandable planning priorities.

The Syria Accountability Act offers another striking illustration of the rejection of the principle of universality. Its core demand refers to UN Security Council Resolution 520, calling for respect for the sovereignty and territorial integrity of Lebanon, violated by Syria because it still retains in Lebanon forces that were welcomed there by the US and Israel in 1976 when their task was to carry out massacres of Palestinians. The congressional legislation, and news reporting and commentary, overlook the fact that Resolution 520, passed in 1982, was explicitly directed against Israel, not Syria, and also the fact that while Israel violated this and other Security Council resolutions regarding Lebanon for twenty-two years, there was no call for any sanctions against Israel, or even any call for reduction in the huge unconditional military and economic aid to Israel. The silence for twenty-two years includes many of those who now signed the Act condemning Syria for its violation of the Security Council resolution ordering Israel to leave Lebanon. The principle is accurately formulated by a rare scholarly commentator, Steven Zunes: it is that "Lebanese sovereignty must be defended only if the occupying army is from a country the United States opposes, but is dispensable if the country is a US ally."[19] The principle, and the news reporting and commentary on all of these events, again make good sense, given the overriding need to reject elementary moral truisms, a fundamental doctrine of the intellectual and moral culture.

Returning to Iraq, when Saddam was removed from the list of states supporting terrorism, Cuba was added to replace it, perhaps in recognition of the sharp escalation in international terrorist attacks against Cuba in the late 1970s, including the bombing of a Cubana airliner killing seventy-three people and many other atrocities. These were mostly planned and implemented in the US, though by that time Washington had moved away from its former policy of direct action in bringing "the terrors of the earth" to Cuba—the goal of the Kennedy administration, reported by historian and Kennedy adviser Arthur Schlesinger in his biography of Robert Kennedy, who was assigned responsibility for the terror campaign and regarded it as a top priority. By the late 1970s, Washington was officially condemning the terrorist acts while harboring and protecting the terrorist cells on US soil in violation of US law. The leading terrorist, Orlando Bosch, regarded as the author of the Cubana airline bombing and dozens of other terrorist acts according to the FBI, was given a presidential pardon by George Bush #1, over the strong objections of the Justice Department. Others like him continue to operate with impunity on US soil, including terrorists responsible for major crimes elsewhere as well for whom the US refuses requests for extradition (from Haiti, for example).

We may recall one of the leading components of the "Bush doctrine"—now Bush #2: "Those who harbor terrorists are as guilty as the terrorists themselves," and must be treated accordingly, the president's words when announcing the bombing of Afghanistan because of its refusal to turn over suspected terrorists to the US, without evidence or even credible pretext as later quietly conceded. Harvard International Relations specialist Graham Allison describes this as the most important component of the Bush Doctrine. It "unilaterally revoked the sovereignty of states that provide sanctuary to terrorists," he wrote approvingly in *Foreign Affairs*, adding that the doctrine has "already become a de facto rule of international relations." That is correct, in the technical sense of "rule of international relations."

Unreconstructed literalists might conclude that Bush and Allison are calling for the bombing of the United States, but that is because they do not comprehend that the most elementary moral truisms must be forcefully rejected: there is a crucial exemption to the principle of universality, so deeply entrenched in the reigning intellectual culture that it is not even perceived, hence not mentioned.

Again, we find illustrations daily. The Negroponte appointment is one example. To take another, a few weeks ago the Palestinian leader Abu Abbas died in a US prison in Iraq. His capture was one of the most heralded achievements of the invasion. A few years earlier he had been living in Gaza, participating in the Oslo "peace process" with US-Israeli approval, but after the second Intifada began, he fled to Baghdad, where he was arrested by the US army and imprisoned because of his role in the hijacking of the cruise ship *Achille Lauro* in 1985. The year 1985 is regarded by scholarship as the peak year of terrorism in the 1980s; Mideast terrorism was the top story of the year, in a poll of editors. Scholarship identifies two major crimes in that year: the hijacking of the *Achille Lauro*, in which one person, a disabled American, was brutally murdered;

and an airplane hijacking with one death, also an American. There were, to be sure, some other terrorist crimes in the region in 1985, but they do not pass through the filters. One was a car bombing outside a mosque in Beirut that killed eighty people and wounded 250 others, timed to explode as people were leaving, killing mostly women and girls; but this is excluded from the record because it was traced back to the CIA and British intelligence.

Another was the action that led to the *Achille Lauro* hijacking in retaliation, a week later: Shimon Peres's bombing of Tunis with no credible pretext, killing seventy-five people, Palestinians and Tunisians, expedited by the US and praised by Secretary of State Shultz, then unanimously condemned by the UN Security Council as an "act of armed aggression" (US abstaining). But that too does not enter the annals of terrorism (or perhaps the more severe crime of "armed aggression"), again because of agency. Peres and Shultz do not die in prison, but receive Nobel prizes, huge taxpayer gifts for reconstruction of what they helped destroy in occupied Iraq, and other honors. Again, it all makes sense once we comprehend that elementary moral truisms must be sent to the flames.

Sometimes denial of moral truisms is explicit. A case in point is the reaction to the second major component of the "Bush Doctrine," formally enunciated in the National Security Strategy of September 2002, which was at once described in the main establishment journal *Foreign Affairs* as a "new imperial grand strategy" declaring Washington's right to resort to force to eliminate any potential challenge to its global dominance. The NSS was widely criticized among the foreign policy elite, including the article just cited, but on narrow grounds: not that it was wrong, or even new, but that the style and implementation were so extreme that they posed threats to US interests. Henry Kissinger described "The new approach [as] revolutionary," pointing out that it undermines the seventeenth-century Westphalian system of international order, and of course the UN Charter and international law. He approved of the doctrine but with reservations about style and tactics, and with a crucial qualification: it cannot be "a universal principle available to every nation." Rather, the right of aggression must be reserved to the US, perhaps delegated to chosen clients. We must forcefully reject the most elementary of moral truisms: the principle of universality. Kissinger is to be praised for his honesty in forthrightly articulating prevailing doctrine, usually concealed in professions of virtuous intent and tortured legalisms.

To add just one last example that is very timely and significant, consider "just war theory," now undergoing a vigorous revival in the context of the "normative revolution" proclaimed in the 1990s. There has been debate about whether the invasion of Iraq satisfies the conditions for just war, but virtually none about the bombing of Serbia in 1999 or the invasion of Afghanistan, taken to be such clear cases that discussion is superfluous. Let us take a quick look at these, not asking whether the attacks were right or wrong, but considering the nature of the arguments.

The harshest criticism of the Serbia bombing anywhere near the mainstream is that it was "illegal but legitimate," the conclusion of the International Independent Commission of Inquiry headed by Justice Richard Goldstone. "It was illegal because it did not receive approval from the UN Security Council," the Commission determined, "but it was legitimate because all diplomatic avenues had been exhausted and there was no other way to stop the killings and atrocities in Kosovo."[20] Justice Goldstone observed that the Charter may need revision in the light of the report and the judgments on which it is based. The NATO intervention, he explains, "is too important a precedent" for it to be regarded "an aberration." Rather, "state sovereignty is being redefined in the fact of globalization and the resolve by the majority of the peoples of the world that human rights have become the business of the international community." He also stressed the need for "objective analysis of human rights abuses."[21]

The last comment is good advice. One question that an objective analysis might address is whether the majority of the peoples of the world accept the judgment of the enlightened states. In the case of the bombing of Serbia, review of the world press and official statements reveals little support for that conclusion, to put it rather mildly. In fact, the bombing was bitterly condemned outside the NATO countries, facts consistently ignored.[22] Furthermore, it is hardly likely that the principled self-exemption of the enlightened states from the "universalization" that traces back to

Nuremberg would gain the approval of much of the world's population. The new norm, it appears, fits the standard pattern.

Another question that objective analysis might address is whether indeed "all diplomatic options had been exhausted." That conclusion is not easy to maintain in the light of the fact that there were two options on the table when NATO decided to bomb—a NATO proposal and a Serbian proposal—and that after seventy-eight days of bombing, a compromise was reached between them.[23]

A third question is whether it is true that "there was no other way to stop the killings and atrocities in Kosovo," clearly a crucial matter. In this case, objective analysis happens to be unusually easy. There is vast documentation available from impeccable Western sources: several compilations of the State Department released in justification of the war, detailed records of the OSCE, NATO, the UN, a British Parliamentary Inquiry, and other similar sources.

There are several remarkable features of the unusually rich documentation. One is that the record is almost entirely ignored in the vast literature on the Kosovo war, including the scholarly literature.[24] The second is that the substantive contents of the documentation are not only ignored, but consistently denied. I have reviewed the record elsewhere, and will not do so here, but what we discover, characteristically, is that the clear and explicit chronology is reversed. The Serbian atrocities are portrayed as the cause of the bombing, whereas it is uncontroversial that they followed it, virtually without exception, and were furthermore its anticipated consequence, as is also well documented from the highest NATO sources.

The British government, the most hawkish element of the alliance, estimated that most of the atrocities were attributable not to the Serbian security forces, but to the KLA guerrillas attacking Serbia from Albania—with the intent, as they frankly explained, to elicit a disproportionate Serbian response that could be used to mobilize Western support for the bombing. The British government assessment was as of mid-January, but the documentary record indicates no substantial change until late March, when the bombing was announced and initiated. The Milošević indictment, based on US and UK intelligence, reveals the same pattern of events.

The US and UK, and commentators generally, cite the Račak massacre in mid-January as the decisive turning point, but that plainly cannot
be taken seriously. First, even assuming the most extreme condemnations
of the Račak massacre to be accurate, it scarcely changed the balance of
atrocities. Second, much worse massacres were taking place at the same
time elsewhere but aroused no concern, though some of the worst could
have easily been terminated merely by withdrawing support.

One notable case in early 1999 is East Timor, under Indonesian military occupation. The US and UK continued to provide their military and
diplomatic support for the occupiers, who had already slaughtered perhaps
one-fourth of the population with unremitting and decisive US-UK support, which continued until well after the Indonesian army virtually destroyed the country in a final paroxysm of violence in August–September
1999. That is only one of many such cases, but it alone more than suffices
to dismiss the professions of horror about Račak.

In Kosovo, Western estimates are that about 2,000 were killed in the
year prior to the invasion. If the British and other assessments are accurate, most of these were killed by the KLA guerrillas. One of the very few
serious scholarly studies even to consider the matter estimates that 500
of the 2,000 were killed by the Serbs. This is the careful and judicious
study by Nicholas Wheeler, who supports the NATO bombing on the
grounds that there would have been worse atrocities had NATO not
bombed.[25] The argument is that by bombing with the anticipation that it
would lead to atrocities, NATO was preventing atrocities, maybe even a
second Auschwitz, many claim. That such arguments are taken seriously,
as they are, gives no slight insight into Western intellectual culture, particularly when we recall that there were diplomatic options and that the
agreement reached after the bombing was a compromise between them
(formally at least).

Justice Goldstone appears to have reservations on this matter as well.
He recognizes—as few do—that the NATO bombing was not undertaken
to protect the Albanian population of Kosovo, and that its "direct result"
was a "tremendous catastrophe" for the Kosovars—as was anticipated by
the NATO command and the State Department, followed by another ca-

tastrophe particularly for Serbs and Roma under NATO-UN occupation. NATO commentators and supporters, Justice Goldstone continues, "have had to console themselves with the belief that 'Operation Horseshoe,' the Serb plan of ethnic cleansing directed against the Albanians in Kosovo, had been set in motion before the bombing began, and not in consequence of the bombing." The word "belief" is appropriate: there is no evidence in the voluminous Western record of anything having been set in motion before the international monitors were withdrawn in preparation for the bombing, and very little in the few days before the bombing began; and "Operation Horseshoe" has since been exposed as an apparent intelligence fabrication, though it can hardly be in doubt that Serbia had contingency plans, at present unknown, for such actions in response to a NATO attack.

It is difficult, then, to see how we can accept the conclusions of the International Commission, a serious and measured effort to deal with the issues, on the legitimacy of the bombing.

The facts are not really controversial, as anyone interested can determine. I suppose that is why the voluminous Western documentary record is so scrupulously ignored. Whatever one's judgment about the bombing, not at issue here, the standard conclusion that it was an uncontroversial example of just war and the decisive demonstration of the "normative revolution" led by the "enlightened states" is, to say the least, rather startling—unless, of course, we return to the same principle: moral truisms must be cast to the flames, when applied to us.

Let us turn to the second case, the war in Afghanistan, considered such a paradigm example of just war that there is scarcely even any discussion about it. The respected moral-political philosopher Jean Bethke Elshtain summarizes received opinion fairly accurately when she writes approvingly that only absolute pacifists and outright lunatics doubt that this was uncontroversially a just war. Here, once again, factual questions arise. First, recall the war aims: to punish Afghans until the Taliban agreed to hand over Osama bin Laden without evidence. Contrary to much subsequent commentary, overthrowing the Taliban regime was an afterthought, added after several weeks of bombing. Second, there is quite good evidence bearing on the belief that only lunatics or absolute pacifists did not join the chorus of approval. An international Gallup poll after the bombing was announced but before it began found very limited support for it, almost none if civilians were targeted, as they were from the first moment. And even that tepid support was based on the presupposition that the targets were known to have been responsible for the September 11 attacks. They were not.

Eight months later, the head of the FBI testified to the Senate that after the most intensive international intelligence inquiry in history, the most that could be said was that the plot was "believed" to have been hatched in Afghanistan, while the attacks were planned and financed elsewhere. It follows that there was no detectable popular support for the bombing, contrary to confident standard claims, apart from a very few countries; and of course Western elites. Afghan opinion is harder to estimate, but we do know that after several weeks of bombing, leading anti-Taliban figures, including some of those most respected by the US and President Karzai, were denouncing the bombing, calling for it to end, and charging the US with bombing just to "show off its muscle" while undermining their efforts to overthrow the Taliban from within.

If we also adopt the truism that facts matter, some problems arise, but there is little fear of that.

Next come the questions of just war. At once, the issue of universality arises. If the US is unquestionably authorized to bomb another country to compel its leaders to turn over someone it suspects of involvement in a terrorist act, then, a fortiori, Cuba, Nicaragua, and a host of others are entitled to bomb the US because there is no doubt of its involvement in very serious terrorist attacks against them: in the case of Cuba going back forty-five years, extensively documented in impeccable sources, and not questioned; in the case of Nicaragua, even condemned by the World Court and the Security Council (in vetoed resolutions), after which the US escalated the attack. This conclusion surely follows if we accept the principle of universality. The conclusion of course is utterly outrageous, and advocated by no one. We therefore conclude, once again, that the principle of universality has a crucial exception, and that rejection of elementary moral truisms is so deeply entrenched that even raising the question is considered an unspeakable abomination. That is yet another instructive comment on the reigning intellectual and moral culture, with its principled rejection of unacceptable platitudes.

The Iraq war has been considered more controversial, so there is an extensive professional literature debating whether it satisfies international law and just war criteria. One distinguished scholar, Michael Glennon of the Fletcher School of Law and Diplomacy, argues forthrightly that international law is simply "hot air" and should be abandoned, because state practice does not conform to it: meaning, the US and its allies ignore it. A further defect of international law and the UN Charter, he argues, is that they limit the capacity of the US to resort to force, and such resort is right and good because the US leads the "enlightened states" (his phrase), apparently by definition: no evidence or argument is adduced, or considered necessary. Another respected scholar argues that the US and UK were in fact acting in accord with the UN Charter, under a "communitarian interpretation" of its provisions: they were carrying out the will of the international community, in a mission implicitly delegated to them because they alone had the power to carry it out.[26] It is apparently irrelevant that the international community vociferously objected, at an unprecedented level—quite evidently, if people are included within the international community, but even among elites.

Others observe that law is a living instrument, its meaning determined by practice, and practice demonstrates that new norms have been established permitting "anticipatory self-defense," another euphemism for aggression at will. The tacit assumption is that norms are established by the powerful, and that they alone have the right of anticipatory self-defense. No one, for example, would argue that Japan exercised this right when it bombed military bases in the US colonies of Hawaii and the Philippines, even though the Japanese knew very well that B-17 Flying Fortresses were coming off the Boeing production lines, and were surely familiar with the very public discussions in the US explaining how they could be used to incinerate Japan's wooden cities in a war of extermination, flying from Hawaiian and Philippine bases.[27] Nor would anyone accord that right to any state today, apart from the self-declared enlightened states, which have the power to determine norms and to apply them selectively at will, basking in praise for their nobility, generosity, and messianic visions of righteousness.

There is nothing particularly novel about any of this, apart from one aspect. The means of destruction that have been developed are by now so awesome, and the risks of deploying and using them so enormous, that a rational Martian observer would not rank the prospects for survival of this curious species very high, as long as contempt for elementary moral truisms remains so deeply entrenched among educated elites.

SIX

Human Intelligence and the Environment*

I'll begin with an interesting debate that took place some years ago between Carl Sagan, the well-known astrophysicist, and Ernst Mayr, the
grand old man of American biology.[1] They were debating the possibility
of finding intelligent life elsewhere in the universe. And Sagan, speaking
from the point of view of an astrophysicist, pointed out that there are in-
numerable planets just like ours. There is no reason they shouldn't have
developed intelligent life. Mayr, from the point of view of a biologist, argued that it's very unlikely that we'll find any. And his reason was, he
said, we have exactly one example: Earth. So let's take a look at Earth.

And what he basically argued is that intelligence is a kind of lethal
mutation. And he had a good argument. He pointed out that if you take
a look at biological success, which is essentially measured by how many
of us are there, the organisms that do quite well are those that mutate
very quickly, like bacteria, or those that are stuck in a fixed ecological
niche, like beetles. They do fine. And they may survive the environmental
crisis. But as you go up the scale of what we call intelligence, they are less
and less successful. By the time you get to mammals, there are very few
of them as compared with, say, insects. By the time you get to humans,

---

*Lecture delivered at The University of North Carolina, Chapel Hill, September 30, 2010.

the origin of humans maybe 100,000 years ago, there is a very small group. We are kind of misled now because there are a lot of humans around, but that's a matter of a few thousand years, which is meaningless from as evolutionary point of view. His argument was, you're just not going to find intelligent life elsewhere, and you probably won't find it here for very long either because it's just a lethal mutation. He also added, a little bit ominously, that the average life span of a species, of the billions that have existed, is about 100,000 years, which is roughly the length of time that the modern humans have existed.

With the environmental crisis, we're now in a situation where we can decide whether Mayr was right or not. If nothing significant is done about it, and pretty quickly, then he will have been correct: human intelligence is indeed a lethal mutation. Maybe some humans will survive, but it will be scattered and nothing like a decent existence, and we'll take a lot of the rest of the living world along with us.

So is anything going to be done about it? The prospects are not very auspicious. There was an international conference on climate change in December 2009.[2] A total disaster. Nothing came out of it. The emerging economies, China, India, and others, argued that it's unfair for them to bear the burden of a couple hundred years of environmental destruction by the currently rich and developed societies. That's a credible argument. But it's one of these cases where you can win the battle and lose the war. The argument isn't going to be very helpful to them if, in fact, the environmental crisis advances and a viable society goes with it. And, of course, the poor countries, for whom they're speaking, will be the worst hit. In fact, they already are the worst hit. That will continue. The rich and developed societies, they split a little bit. Europe is actually doing something about it; it's done some things to level off emissions. The United States has not.

In fact, there is a well-known environmentalist writer, George Monbiot, who wrote after the Copenhagen conference, "The immediate reason for the failure of the talks can be summarised in two words: Barack Obama."[3] And he's correct. Obama's intervention in the conference was, of course, very significant, given the power and the role of the United

States in any international event. And he basically killed it. No restrictions, the Kyoto Protocols die. The United States never participated in it. Emissions have very sharply increased in the United States since, and nothing is being done to curb it. A few Band-Aids here and there, but basically nothing. Of course, it's not just Barack Obama. It's our whole society and culture. Our institutions are constructed in such a way that trying to achieve anything is going to be extremely difficult.

What's particularly interesting is the role of the corporate sector, which pretty much runs the country and the political system. They're very explicit. The big business lobbies, like the Chamber of Commerce, American Petroleum Institute, and others, have been very clear and explicit. They have been carrying out a major publicity campaign to convince people that climate change is not real, that it's a liberal hoax. It's particularly interesting to take a look at the people who are running these campaigns, say, the CEOs of big corporations. They know as well as you and I do that it's very real and that the threats are very dire, and that they're threatening the lives of their grandchildren. In fact, they're threatening what they own: they own the world, and they're threatening its survival. This seems irrational, and it is, from a certain perspective. But from another perspective it's highly rational. They're acting within the structure of the institutions of which they are a part. They are functioning within something like market systems—not quite, but partially—market systems. To the extent that you participate in a market system, you disregard necessarily what economists call "externalities," the effect of a transaction upon others. So, for example, if one of you sells me a car, we may try to make a good deal for ourselves, but we don't take into account in that transaction the effect of the transaction on others. Of course, there is an effect. It may feel like a small effect, but if it multiplies over a lot of people it's a huge effect: pollution, congestion, wasting time in traffic jams, all sorts of things. Those you don't take into account—necessarily. That's part of the market system.

We've just been through a major illustration of this. The financial crisis has many roots, but its fundamental root has been known for a long time. It was talked about decades before the crisis. In fact, there have been repeated crises. This is just the worst of them. The fundamental reason is rooted in market systems. If Goldman Sachs, say, makes a transaction, if they're doing their job, if the managers are up to speed and are paying attention to what they get out of it and the institution or person at the other end of the transaction, say, a borrower, does the same thing, they don't take into account what's called systemic risk, that is, the chance that the transaction that they're carrying out will contribute to crashing the whole system. They don't take that into account. In fact, that's a large part of what just happened. The systemic risk turned out to be huge, enough to crash the system. Even though the original transactions are perfectly rational within the system.

It's not because they're bad people or anything. If they don't do it—suppose some CEO says, "Okay, I'm going to take into account externalities"—then he's out. He's out and somebody else is in. That's the nature of the institution. You can be a perfectly nice guy in your personal life. You can sign up for the Sierra Club, and give speeches about the environmental crisis or whatever, but in the role of corporate manager you're fixed. You have to try to maximize short-term profit and market share—in fact, that's a legal requirement in Anglo-American corporate law—because if you don't do it, either your business will disappear because somebody else will outperform it in the short run, or you will just be out because you're not doing your job and somebody else will be in. So there is an institutional irrationality. Within the institution the behavior is perfectly rational, but the institutions themselves are so totally irrational that they are designed to crash.

If you look, say, at the financial system, it's extremely dramatic, what happened. There was a crash in the 1920s and the 1930s, a huge depression. But then regulatory mechanisms were introduced. They were introduced as a result of massive popular pressure, but they were introduced. And throughout the whole period of very rapid and pretty egalitarian economic growth of the next couple of decades, there were no financial crises, because the regulatory mechanisms interfered with the market and prevented the market principles from operating. So therefore you could take account of externalities. That's what the regulatory system does.

First of all, the role of finance in the economy has exploded, so the share of corporate profit by financial institutions has just zoomed since the 1970s. A corollary to that expansion has been the hollowing out of industrial production, sending it abroad. This has all happened under the impact of the kind of fanatic religious ideology called neoclassical economics—hypotheses that have no theoretical grounds and no empirical support but are very attractive because you can prove theorems if you adopt them: the efficient market hypothesis, rational expectations hypothesis, and so on. The spread of these ideologies, which is very attractive to concentrated wealth and privilege, hence their success, was epitomized in Alan Greenspan, who at least had the decency to say it was all wrong when it collapsed.[4] I don't think there has ever been a collapse of an intellectual edifice comparable to this in history—at least, I can't remember one. Interestingly, it has no effect. It just continues. Which tells you that somehow it's serviceable to power systems.

Under the impact of these ideologies, the regulatory system was dismantled by Reagan and Clinton and Bush. Throughout this whole period there have been repeated financial crises, unlike in the 1950s and 1960s. During the Reagan years there were some really extreme ones. Clinton left office with another huge one, the burst of the tech bubble. Then the one we're in the middle of. Worse and worse each time. The system is instantly being reconstructed, so the next one will very likely be even worse. One of the causes, not the only one, is simply the fact that in market systems you just don't take into account externalities, in this case systemic risk.

That's not lethal in the case of financial crises. A financial crisis can be terrible. It can put many millions of people out of work and destroy their lives. But there is a way out of it. The taxpayer can come in and rescue you. That's exactly what happened. We saw it dramatically in the last couple of years. The financial system tanked. The government, namely, the taxpayer, came in and bailed them out. But there's nobody around to bail you out of an environmental crisis. The externalities in this case are the fate of the species. If that's disregarded in the operations of the market system, there's nobody around who is going to bail you out from that. So this is a lethal externality. And the fact that it's proceeding with no significant action being taken to do anything about it does suggest that Ernst Mayr actually had a point. That there is something about us, our intelligence, that we're capable of acting in ways that are rational within a narrow framework but are irrational in terms of other long-term goals, like do we care what kind of a world our grandchildren will live in. And it's hard to see much in the way of prospects for overcoming this right now, particularly in the United States. We are the most powerful state in the world, and what we do is vastly important. We have one of the worst records in this regard.

There are things that could be done. It's not hard to list them. One of the main things that could be done, for example, is the weatherization of homes. There was a big building boom in the post–Second World War period, and from the point of view of the environment, it was done extremely irrationally. Again, it was done rationally from a market point of view. There were models for home building, for mass-produced homes, which were used all over the country, under different conditions. So maybe it would make sense in Arizona, but not in Massachusetts. Those homes are there. They're extremely energy-inefficient. They can be fixed. It's construction work, basically. It would make a big difference. It would also have the effect of reviving one of the main collapsing industries, construction, and overcoming a substantial part of the employment crisis. It will take inputs. It will take money from, ultimately, the taxpayer. (We call it the government, but it means the taxpayer.) But it would be a way of stimulating the economy, increasing jobs, and also making a significant impact on the destruction of the environment. But there's barely a proposal for this, almost nothing.

Another example, which is kind of a scandal in the United States— if any of you have traveled abroad, you're perfectly aware of it—when you come back from almost anywhere in the world to the United States, it looks like you're coming to a Third World country, literally. The infrastructure is collapsing, transportation doesn't work. Let's just take trains. When I moved to Boston around 1950, there was a train that went from Boston to New York. It took three hours and forty-five minutes. There's now a highly heralded train called the Acela, the super train. It takes three hours and thirty minutes. If you were in Japan, Germany, China, almost anywhere, it would take maybe two hours. And that's general.

This didn't happen by accident. It happened by a huge social engineering project carried out by the government and by the corporations beginning in the 1940s. It was a very systematic effort to redesign the society so as to maximize the use of fossil fuels. One part of it was eliminating quite efficient rail systems. New England, for example, did have a pretty efficient electric rail system all the way through New England. If you read E. L. Doctorow's novel *Ragtime*, the first chapter describes its hero going through New England on the electric rail system.[5] That was all dismantled in favor of cars and trucks. Los Angeles, which is now a total horror story—I don't know if any of you have been there—had an efficient electric public transportation system. It was dismantled. It was bought up in the 1940s by General Motors, Firestone Rubber, and Standard Oil of California. The purpose of their buying it up was to dismantle it so as to shift everything to trucks and cars and buses. And it was done. It was technically a conspiracy. Actually, they were brought to court on a charge of conspiracy and sentenced. I think the sentence was around $5,000, enough to pay for the victory dinner.[6]

The federal government stepped in. We have something that is now called the interstate highway system. When it was built in the 1950s, it was called the national defense highway system because when you do anything in the United States, you have to call it defense. That's the only way you can fool the taxpayer into paying for it. In fact, there were stories back in the 1950s, those of you who are old enough to remember, about how we needed it because you had to move missiles around the country very quickly in case the Russians came or something. So taxpayers were bilked into paying for this system. Alongside of it was the destruction of railroads, which is why you have what I just described. Huge amounts of federal money and corporate money went into highways, airports. Anything that wastes fuel. That's basically the criterion.

Also, the country was suburbanized. Real estate interests, local interests, and others redesigned life so that it's atomized and suburbanized. I'm not knocking the suburbs. I live in one and I like it. But it's incredibly in-efficient. It has all kinds of social effects that are probably deleterious.

Anyway, it didn't just happen; it was designed. Throughout the whole period there has been a massive effort to create the most destructive pos-sible society. And to try to redo that huge social engineering project is not going to be simple. It involves plenty of problems.

Another component of any reasonable approach—and everyone on paper agrees with this—is to develop sustainable energy, green technol-ogy. We all know and everyone talks a nice line about that. But if you look at what's happening, green technology is being developed in Spain, in Germany, and primarily in China. The United States is importing it. In fact, a lot of the innovation is here, but it's done there. US investors now are putting more money into green technology in China than into the United States and Europe combined. There were complaints when Texas ordered solar panels and windmills from China: "It's undermining our industry." Actually, it wasn't undermining us at all, because we were out of the game. It was undermining Spain and Germany, which are way ahead of us.

Just to indicate how surreal this is, the Obama administration es-sentially took over the auto industry—meaning *you* took it over. You paid for it, bailed it out, and basically own it. And they continued doing ex-actly what the corporations had been doing pretty much, for example, closing down GM plants all over the place. Closing down a plant is not just putting the workers out of work; it's also destroying the community. Take a look at the so-called rust belt. The communities were built by labor organizing; they developed around the plants. Now they're disman-tled. It has huge effects. At the same time that they're dismantling the plants, meaning you and I are dismantling plants, because that's where the money comes from, and it's allegedly our representatives—it isn't, in fact—at the very same time Obama was sending his Transportation Sec-retary to Spain to use federal stimulus money to get contracts for high-speed rail construction, which we really need and the world really needs.[7] Those plants that are being dismantled and the skilled workers in them, all that could be reconverted to producing high-speed rail right here.

They have the technology, they have the knowledge, they have the skills. But it's not good for the bottom line for banks, so we'll buy it from Spain. Just like green technology, it will be done in China.

Those are choices; those are not laws of nature. But, unfortunately, those are the choices that are being made. And there is little indication of any positive change. These are pretty serious problems. We can easily go on. I don't want to continue. But the general picture is very much like this. I don't think this is an unfair selection of—it's a selection, of course, but I think it's a reasonably fair selection of what's happening. The consequences are pretty dire.

The media contribute to this, too. So if you read, say, a typical story in the *New York Times*, it will tell you that there is a debate about global warming. If you look at the debate, on one side is maybe 98 percent of the relevant scientists in the world, on the other side are a couple of serious scientists who question it, a handful, and Jim Inhofe or some other senator. So it's a debate. And the citizen has to kind of make a decision between these two sides. The *Times* had an almost hysterical front-page article in which the headline said that meteorologists question global warming.[8] It discussed a debate between meteorologists—the meteorologists are these pretty faces who read what somebody hands to them on television and say it's going to rain tomorrow. That's one side of the debate. The other side of the debate is practically every scientist who knows anything about it. Again, the citizen is supposed to decide. Do I trust these meteorologists? They tell me whether to wear a raincoat tomorrow. And what do I know about the scientists? They're sitting in some laboratory somewhere with a computer model. So, yes, people are confused, and understandably.

It's interesting that these debates leave out almost entirely a third part of the debate, namely, a very substantial number of scientists, competent scientists, who think that the scientific consensus is much too optimistic. A group of scientists at MIT came out with a report about a year ago describing what they called in the scientific publications the most comprehensive modeling of the climate that had ever been done.[9] Their conclusion, which was unreported, except for the science journals, was that the major scientific consensus of the international commission is just way off, it's much too optimistic; and if you add other factors that they didn't count in properly, the conclusion is much more dire. Their own conclusion was that unless we terminate use of fossil fuels almost immediately, it's finished. We'll never be able to overcome the consequences. That's not part of the debate.

I could easily go on, but the only counterweight is a very substantial popular movement that is not just going to call for just putting solar panels on your roof—though it's a good thing to do—but will have to dismantle an entire sociological, cultural, economic, and ideological structure that is just driving us to disaster. It's not a small task, but it's a task that had better be undertaken, and pretty quickly, or it's going to be too late.

SEVEN

Can Civilization Survive
Really Existing Capitalism?*

In referring to "really existing capitalism," I have in mind what really exists and what is called "capitalism." The United States is the most important case, for obvious reasons.

The term "capitalism" is vague enough to cover many possibilities. It is commonly used to refer to the US economic system, which receives substantial state intervention, ranging from creative innovation to the "too-big-to-fail" government insurance policy for banks, and which is highly monopolized, further limiting market reliance, increasingly so.

It's worth bearing in mind the scale of the departures of "really existing capitalism" from official "free-market capitalism." To mention only a few examples, in the past twenty years, the share of profits of the two hundred largest enterprises has risen sharply, carrying forward the oligopolistic character of the US economy.[1] This directly undermines markets, avoiding price wars through efforts at often-meaningless product differentiation through massive advertising, which is itself dedicated to undermining markets in the official sense, based on informed consumers making rational choices. Computers and the Internet, along with other basic components of the IT revolution, were largely in the state sector

---

*Inaugural Lecture delivered at University College Dublin Philosophy Society, April 2, 2013.

(R&D, subsidy, procurement, and other devices) for decades before they were handed over to private enterprise for adaptation to commercial markets and profit. The government insurance policy that provides big banks with enormous advantages has been roughly estimated by economists and the business press to be on the order of some $40 billion a year. However, a recent study by the International Monetary Fund indicates—to quote the business press—that perhaps "the largest US banks aren't really profitable at all," adding that "the billions of dollars they allegedly earn for their shareholders were almost entirely a gift from US taxpayers."[2] This is more evidence to support the judgment of the most respected financial correspondent in the English-speaking world, Martin Wolf of the London *Financial Times*, that "an out-of-control financial sector is eating out the modern market economy from inside, just as the larva of the spider wasp eats out the host in which it has been laid."[3]

The term "capitalism" is also commonly used for systems in which there are no capitalists: for example, the extensive worker-owned Mondragón conglomerate in the Basque Country of Spain or the worker-owned enterprises expanding in northern Ohio—often with conservative support—a matter discussed in important work by Gar Alperovitz.[4] Some might even use the term "capitalism" to include the industrial democracy advocated by John Dewey, America's leading social philosopher. He called for workers to be "masters of their own industrial fate," and for all institutions to be under public control, including the means of production, exchange, publicity, transportation, and communication.[5] Short of this, Dewey argued, politics will remain "the shadow cast on society by big business."[6]

The truncated democracy that Dewey condemned has been left in tatters in recent years. Now, control of government is narrowly concentrated at the peak of the income scale, while the large majority "down below" are virtually disenfranchised. The current political-economic system is a form of plutocracy that diverges sharply from democracy, if by that concept we mean political arrangements in which policy is significantly influenced by the public will.

There have been serious debates over the years about whether capitalism is, in principle, compatible with democracy. If we keep to really existing capitalist democracy—RECD for short (pronounced "wrecked")—the question is effectively answered: they are radically incompatible. For reasons to which I'll return, it seems to me unlikely that civilization can survive really existing capitalism and the sharply attenuated democracy that goes along with it. Could functioning democracy make a difference? Consideration of nonexistent systems can only be speculative, but I think there's some reason to think so.

Let's keep to the most critical immediate problem that civilization faces, though not the only one: environmental catastrophe. Policies and public attitudes diverge sharply, as is often the case under RECD. The nature of the gap is examined in several articles in the current issue of *Daedalus*, the journal of the American Academy of Arts and Sciences. The researchers find that "109 countries have enacted some form of policy regarding renewable power, and 118 countries have set targets for renewable energy. In contrast, the United States has not adopted any consistent and stable set of policies at the national level to foster the use of renewable energy."[7]

It is not public opinion that drives policy off the international spectrum—quite the opposite. The public is much closer to the global norm than policy. It is also much more supportive of actions to confront the likely environmental disaster predicted by an overwhelming scientific consensus—and it is not too far off; in the lives of our grandchildren, very likely. As the *Daedalus* researchers found:

> Huge majorities have favored steps by the federal government to reduce the amount of greenhouse gas emissions generated when utilities produce electricity. In 2006, 86 percent of respondents favored requiring utilities, or encouraging them with tax breaks, to reduce the amount of greenhouse gases they emit. . . . Also in that year, 87 percent favored tax breaks for utilities that produce more electricity from water, wind, or sunlight. . . . These majorities were maintained between 2006 and 2010 and shrank somewhat after that.[8]

The fact that the public is influenced by science is deeply troubling to those who dominate the economy and state policy. One current illustration of their concern is the Environmental Literacy Improvement Act being proposed to legislatures by ALEC, the American Legislative Exchange Council, a corporate-funded lobby that designs legislation to serve the needs of the corporate sector and extreme wealth. The ALEC act mandates "balanced" teaching of climate science in K–12 classrooms. "Balanced teaching" is a code phrase that refers to teaching climate-change denial in order to "balance" mainstream climate science. It is analogous to the "balanced teaching" advocated by creationists to enable the teaching of "creation science" in public schools.[9] Legislation based on ALEC models has already been introduced in several states.

The ALEC legislation is based on a project of the Heartland Institute, a corporate-funded think tank dedicated to rejecting the scientific consensus on the climate. The Heartland Institute project calls for a "Global Warming Curriculum for K-12 Classrooms" that aims to teach that there "is a major controversy over whether or not humans are changing the weather."[10] Of course, all of this is dressed up in rhetoric about teaching critical thinking—a fine idea, no doubt, but it's easy to think up far better choices than an issue selected because of its importance for corporate profits.

There is indeed a controversy, regularly reported in the media. One side consists of the overwhelming majority of scientists, all of the world's major national academies of science, the professional science journals, and the IPCC (the Intergovernmental Panel on Climate Change). They agree that global warming is taking place; that there is a substantial human component; that the situation is serious and perhaps dire; and that very soon, maybe within decades, the world might reach a tipping point where the process will escalate sharply and will be irreversible, with severe social and economic effects. It is rare to find such consensus on complex scientific issues.

The other side consists of skeptics, including a few respected scientists who caution that much is unknown—which means that things might not be as bad as thought, or might be worse.

Omitted from the contrived debate is a much larger group of skeptics: highly regarded climate scientists who regard the regular reports of the IPCC as much too conservative. They have repeatedly been proven correct, unfortunately. But they are scarcely part of the public debate, though very prominent in the scientific literature.

The Heartland Institute and ALEC are part of a huge campaign by corporate lobbies to sow doubt about the near-unanimous consensus of scientists that human activities are having a major impact on global warming with possibly ominous implications. The campaign was openly announced and includes the lobbying organizations of the fossil-fuel industry, the American Chamber of Commerce (the main business lobby), and others. The efforts of ALEC and the famous Koch brothers, are, however, a fraction of what is underway. The initiatives are concealed in complex ways but are sometimes partially revealed, for example in a current report by Suzanne Goldenberg in the London *Guardian,* which finds that "conservative billionaires used a secretive funding route to channel nearly $120 million . . . to more than 100 groups casting doubt about the science behind climate change," helping to "build a vast network of think tanks and activist groups working to a single purpose: to redefine climate change from neutral scientific fact to a highly polarizing 'wedge issue' for hardcore conservatives."[11]

The propaganda campaign has apparently had some effect on US public opinion, which is more skeptical than the global norm. But the effect is not significant enough to satisfy the masters. That is presumably why sectors of the corporate world are launching their attack on the educational system in an effort to counter the dangerous tendency of the public to pay attention to the conclusions of scientific research.

At the Republican National Committee's winter meeting a few weeks ago, Governor Bobby Jindal warned the leadership "we must stop being the stupid party. . . . We must stop insulting the intelligence of voters."[12] ALEC and its corporate backers, in contrast, want the country to be "the stupid nation"—and for principled reasons.

One of the dark-money organizations of billionaires funding climate-change denial is Donors Trust, which is also a major contributor to efforts to deny voting rights to poor Blacks. That makes sense. African-Americans tend to be Democrats, even social democrats, and might even go so far as to pay attention to science, unlike those properly trained to think critically by "balanced" teaching.

The major science journals regularly give a sense of how surreal all of this is. Take *Science*, the major US scientific weekly. In the January 18, 2013, issue it had three news items side by side. One reported that 2012 was the hottest year on record in the US, continuing a long trend. The second reported a new study by the US Global Climate Change Research Program that provided additional evidence for rapid climate change as the result of human activities and discussed likely severe impacts. The third reported the new appointments to chair the committees on science policy chosen by the House of Representatives, where a minority of voters elected a large majority of Republicans thanks to the shredding of the political system. All three of the new chairs deny that humans contribute to climate change, two deny that it is even taking place, and one is a longtime advocate for the fossil fuel industry. The same issue of the journal has a technical article with new evidence that the irreversible tipping point may be ominously close.[13]

Another report in *Science* from January 2013 underscores the need to ensure that we become the stupid nation.[14] The report provides evidence that even slightly warmer temperatures, less of a rise than is currently anticipated in coming years, could start melting permafrost, which in turn could trigger the release of huge amounts of greenhouse gases trapped in ice. Best to keep to "balanced education"—if, that is, we can face the grandchildren whose lives we are busy destroying.

Within RECD it is of extreme importance that we become the stupid nation, not misled by science and rationality, in the interests of the short-term gains of the masters of the economy and political system, damn the consequences. These commitments are deeply rooted in the market-fundamentalist doctrines that are preached within RECD but are observed in a highly selective manner, so as to sustain a powerful state to serve wealth and power—what economist Dean Baker calls a "conservative nanny state."[15]

The official doctrines suffer from a number of familiar "market inefficiencies," among them the failure to count the effects on others in market transactions. The consequences of these "externalities" can be substantial. The current financial crisis is an illustration: it is partly traceable to ignoring "systemic risk"—the possibility that the whole system will collapse—when the major banks and investment firms undertake risky and hence profitable transactions. Environmental catastrophe is far more serious: the externalities being ignored include the fate of the species. And there is nowhere to run, cap in hand, for a bailout.

These consequences have deep roots in RECD and its guiding doctrines, which also dictate that the masters should exert major efforts to escalate the threats. This is one reason—not the only one—why it seems unlikely that civilization will survive RECD without severe blows.

A future historian would look back on a curious spectacle taking shape in the early twenty-first century. For the first time in human history, humans are facing significant prospects of severe calamity, as a result of their own actions, that are battering the foundations of decent survival. There is a range of reactions. At one extreme, some seek to act decisively to prevent possible catastrophe. At the other extreme, major efforts are underway to deny what is happening and to dumb down the population so that they won't interfere with short-term profit. Leading the effort to intensify the likely disaster is the richest and most powerful country in world history and the most prominent example of RECD, with incomparable advantages. Leading the effort to preserve conditions in which our immediate descendants might have a decent life are the so-called "primitive" societies: First Nations, tribal, indigenous, aboriginal.

The countries with large and influential indigenous populations are well in the lead in seeking to preserve the planet. The countries that have driven indigenous populations to extinction or extreme marginalization are racing forward enthusiastically toward destruction. Thus Ecuador, with a large indigenous population, is seeking aid from the rich countries to allow it to keep its substantial oil reserves underground, where they should be. Meanwhile, the US and Canada enthusiastically seek to burn fossil fuels, including the extremely dangerous Canadian tar sands, and to do so as quickly and fully as possible while they hail the wonders of a century of (largely meaningless) energy independence without a side glance at what the world might look like after this extravagant commitment to self-destruction.

The observation generalizes. Throughout the world, indigenous societies are struggling to protect what they sometimes call "the rights of
nature," while the civilized and sophisticated scoff at this silliness.

All exactly the opposite of what rationality would predict—unless it is
the skewed form of reason that passes through the distorting filter of RECD.

Notes

EPIGRAPH

1. Adam Smith, *The Wealth of Nations* (Oxford: Clarendon Press, 1976), Book III, chapter 4, p. 418.

FOREWORD BY MARCUS RASKIN

1. Noam Chomsky, "The Responsibility of Intellectuals," in *The Essential Chomsky*, ed. Anthony Arnove (New York: The New Press, 2008), p. 40.
2. Noam Chomsky, *On Power and Ideology: The Managua Lectures* (Boston: South End Press, 1987), p. 140. (A new edition of this work is forthcoming in 2015 from Haymarket Books.)
3. Samuel Arthur Jones, *Thoreau's Incarceration, As Told by His Jailer* (Berkeley Heights, NJ: Oriole Press, 1962), p. 18. Samuel Arthur Jones and George Hendrick, *Thoreau Amongst Friends and Philistines, and Other Thoreauviana* (Athens, OH: Ohio University Press, 1982), pp. xxvi and 241.
4. See Piero Gleijeses, *Shattered Hope: The Guatemalan Revolution and the United States, 1944–1954* (Princeton, NJ: Princeton University Press, 1991).
5. Noam Chomsky and Edward S. Herman, *The Political Economy of Human Rights, Volume I: The Washington Connection and Third World Fascism* (Boston: South End Press, 1979), p. 100. (A new edition of this work is forthcoming in 2014 from Haymarket Books.)
6. Noam Chomsky, "Foreign Policy and the Intelligentsia," in *The Essential Chomsky*, p. 167.
7. See Gabriel Kolko, *The Politics of War: The World and United States Foreign Policy, 1943–1945* (New York: Random House, 1968); Joyce Kolko and Gabriel Kolko, *The Limits of Power: The World and United States Foreign Policy, 1945–1954* (New York: Harper & Row, 1972); Denna Frank Fleming, *The Cold War and Its Origins,*

1917–1960 (Garden City, NY: Doubleday, 1961); and Laurence H. Shoup and William Minter, *Imperial Brain Trust: The Council on Foreign Relations and United States Foreign Policy* (New York: Monthly Review Press, 1977).

8. Chomsky, "The Responsibility of Intellectuals," in *The Essential Chomsky*, pp. 39–62.

9. See V. G. Kiernan, *America: The New Imperialism; From White Settlement to World Hegemony* (London: Zed, 1978); Walter LaFeber, *The New Empire: An Interpretation of American Expansion, 1860–1898* (Ithaca, NY: Cornell University Press, 1963); Richard Warner Van Alstyne, *The Rising American Empire* (New York: Norton, 1974); William Appleman Williams, *The Tragedy of American Diplomacy*, 2nd ed. (New York: Dell, 1972); and William Appleman Williams, *The Contours of American History* (New York: Norton, 1988).

ONE: KNOWLEDGE AND POWER: INTELLECTUALS AND THE WELFARE-WARFARE STATE

1. The quotes are from various essays collected in Carl Resek, ed., *War and the Intellectuals* (New York: Harper, 1964).

2. In Richard M. Feffer, ed., *No More Vietnams? The War and the Future of American Foreign Policy* (New York: Harper, 1968). [Thomson's italics.] The phrase "technocracy's own Bolsheviks" would perhaps be more apt, given the actual role of Mao in opposing the party bureaucracy and in the conflict of "red" and "expert," particularly in the past few years. There is a substantial literature on the latter topic. See, for example, Benjamin Schwartz, "The Reign of Virtue: Some Broad Perspectives on Leader and Party in the Cultural Revolution," *China Quarterly*, July 1968. He stresses Mao's opposition to the "technocratic element" and his attempt to realize "the concept of the masses as active and total participants in the whole political process" under the guidance of an "ethical elite" that acts as a "moralizing agency" in the society, "transform[ing] the people below them through the power of example, education and proper policy." I return to this matter briefly below.

3. John K. Galbraith, *The New Industrial State* (New York: Houghton Mifflin, 1967).

4. Barrington Moore Jr., "Revolution in America?," *New York Review of Books*, January 30, 1969.

5. Barrington Moore Jr., "Thoughts on Violence and Democracy," *Proceedings of the Academy of Political Science* 29, no. 1 (1968); Robert H. Connery, ed., *Urban Riots: Violence and Social Change* (New York: Vintage Books, 1969).

6. Melvin Laird, *A House Divided: America's Strategy Gap* (Washington, DC: Henry Regnery, 1962). Not surprisingly, he concludes: "Step one of a military strategy of initiative should be the credible announcement of our determination to strike first if necessary to protect our vital interests." Only in this way can we exercise our "moral responsibility to use our power constructively to prevent Communism from destroying the heritage of our world civilization." See *I. F. Stone's Weekly*, December 30, 1968, for additional quotations from this amazing document. Compare *New York Times* military expert Hanson Baldwin, who urges that in the post-Vietnam era we be prepared to "escalate technologically" rather than with manpower" when we find it difficult to "bolster governments under attack and secure them against

creeping Communism": "Such escalation might involve the use of exotic new conventional weapons, or the utilization under carefully restricted conditions, where
targets and geography are favorable, of small nuclear devices for *defensive* purposes"
(*New York Times Magazine*, June 9, 1968). Particularly interesting is the concept of
"defensive purposes"—as we bolster a weak government against creeping Communism. As far as I know, this is the only country where the minister of war has spoken
in favor of a possible preventive war and the leading military expert of the press
has advocated first use of nuclear weapons.

7. For some discussion, see my *American Power and the New Mandarins* (New York:
Pantheon, 1969), particularly chapter 3, "The Logic of Withdrawal." (The book
was republished by The New Press in 2002.)

8. Moore Jr., "Revolution in America?"

9. In a number of respects. For example, a war that demands a shift of government
spending to boots and bullets fails to benefit the technologically advanced seg-
ments of the economy, a fact that has been noted by many. Compare, for example,
Michael Kidron, *Western Capitalism since the War* (London: Weidenfeld and
Nicholson, 1968), who comments on "the technologically-regressive impact of the
Vietnam war with its reversion to *relatively* labor-intensive products."

10. For a remarkably cynical example, see the comments of Ithiel Pool in Feffer, ed.,
No More Vietnams?—and for his own interpretations of these remarks, *New York
Review of Books*, letters, February 16, 1969.

11. Peter Kropotkin, *The State: Its Historic Role* [1896] (London: Freedom Press, 1911).

12. Mikhail Bakunin, *The State and Anarchy*, cited by Daniel Guèrin in *Jeunesse du
socialisme libertaire* (Paris: Marcel Rivière, 1959).

13. Letter to Aleksandr Herzen and Nikolai Ogareff [Ogarev], 1866, cited by Guèrin,
Jeunesse du socialisme libertaire.

14. See, for example, the informative essay by Daniel Bell, "Two Roads from Marx,"
reprinted in his book *The End of Ideology: On the Exhaustion of Political Ideas in
the Fifties* (New York: Free Press, 1960).

15. Rosa Luxemburg, *The Russian Revolution*, written in prison in 1918.

16. Reprinted in English translation together with *The Russian Revolution* in a volume
edited by Bertram Wolfe: Rosa Luxemburg, *The Russian Revolution and Leninism or
Marxism?* (Ann Arbor: University of Michigan Press, 1961). [Luxemburg's italics.]

17. In 1918, she of course makes no mention of the functionary who later became dic-
tator of the Russian state, realizing these fears to an extreme that no one anticipated.

18. The closing words of Rosa Luxemburg, *Leninism or Marxism?*

19. In the latter connection, see Michael Rogin's excellent critique of "The Pluralist
Defense of Modern Industrial Society" in contemporary liberal sociology: Michael
Paul Rogin, *The Intellectuals and McCarthy: The Radical Specter* (Cambridge, MA:
MIT Press, 1967).

20. For some discussion of both the events and the response see my *American Power
and the New Mandarins*, chapter 1, "Objectivity and Liberal Scholarship."

21. A concise and useful review is presented in George Zaninovich, *The Development
of Socialist Yugoslavia* (Baltimore, MD: Johns Hopkins University Press, 1968).

22. William Hinton, *Fanshen* (New York: Monthly Review Press, 1966)—a book that

would have appeared many years before had it not been for the scandalous behavior of US customs officials and the Senate Internal Security Committee, who released Hinton's impounded notes only after a lengthy and costly legal battle.

23. Douglas Pike, *Vietcong* (Cambridge, MA: MIT Press, 1966). As a work of propaganda, this book is of course tainted from the start. But it gains a certain credibility from the fact that it presents a remarkably powerful argument-against-interest, apparently without the author understanding this.

24. For example, the eyewitness accounts of journalist Katsuichi Honda published in the *Asahi Shimbun* in 1967 and translated into English: *The National Liberation Front*, in the series *Vietnam—A Voice from the Villages*, c/o Room 506, Shinwa Building, Sakuraga-oka-4, Shibuya-ku, Tokyo.

25. In this connection, an example of major importance is provided by the Palestinian (later Israeli) Kibbutzim. For analysis and discussion, see Haim Darin-Drabkin, *The Other Society* (New York: Harcourt, Brace & World, 1962). The significance of these cooperative forms has largely been missed by the left for two reasons: first, the social and economic success of the Kibbutzim seems unimportant to the "radical centralizers" who see the move toward socialism as a matter of acquisition of power by a revolutionary vanguard (in the name of . . . , etc.); and second, the matter is complicated by a factor that is irrelevant to the question of the Kibbutz as a social form, namely, the problems of national conflict in the Middle East (it is useful—though again basically irrelevant to the Kibbutz as a social form—to recall that until 1947 the left wing of the Kibbutz movement, a substantial movement, was opposed to the idea of a Jewish state, correctly, in my opinion).

26. One of the "infantile ultra-leftists" discussed by Lenin in his pamphlet of 1920. For a comparison of Lenin's views before and after the acquisition of state power, see Robert Daniels, "The State and Revolution: A Case Study in the Genesis and Transformation of Communist Ideology," *American Slavic and East European Review*, February 1953. He emphasizes Lenin's "intellectual deviation" to the left "during the year of revolution, 1917." Arthur Rosenberg's *A History of Bolshevism: From Marx to the First Five-Years' Plan* [1932] (New York: Doubleday 1965), which remains, to my mind, the outstanding study of this topic, presents a more sympathetic view, recognizing Lenin's political realism while pointing out the basically authoritarian character of his thought. For more on this subject, see Robert Daniels, *The Conscience of the Revolution: Communist Opposition in Soviet Russia* (Cambridge, MA: Harvard University Press, 1960), and a useful collection edited by Helmut Gruber, *International Communism in the era of Lenin: A Documentary History* (Ithaca, NY: Cornell University Press, 1967); and other sources too numerous to mention.

27. Anton Pannekoek, *Lenin as Philosopher*, first published in Amsterdam under the pseudonym John Harper as *Lenin als Philosoph. Kritische Betrachtung der philosophischen Grundlagen des Leninismus*, in Bibliothek der Rätekorrespondenz, No.1, Ausgabe der Gruppe Internationaler Kommunisten, 1938. The date is important for understanding the specific references.

28. Zbigniew Brzezinski, "America in the Technetronic Age," *Encounter*, January 1968. A number of citations with similar content are given in Leonard S. Silk, "Business

Power, Today and Tomorrow," *Daedalus*, Winter 1969. Silk, chairman of the editorial board of *Business Week*, takes a rather skeptical view of the prospects for transfer of corporate power to a "bureaucracy of technicians," expecting rather that, useful as the technostructure may be, business will maintain its socially dominant role. The only question of this sort seriously at issue, in this study of the American Academy of Arts and Sciences, is the relative power of owners, management, and technostructure in control of the corporation. Popular control of economic institutions is of course not discussed.

29. Alfred D. Chandler Jr., "The Role of Business in the United States: A Historical Survey," *Daedelus*, Winter 1969.

30. Chandler, "The Role of Business in the United States." The experience prompted the following remark by Paul Samuelson: "It has been said that the last year was the chemist's war and that this one is the physicist's. It might equally be said that this is an economist's war." *New Republic*, September 11, 1944. Cited in Robert Lekachman, *The Age of Keynes* (New York: Random House, 1966). Perhaps we might regard the Vietnam War as another "economist's war," given the role of professional economists in helping maintain domestic stability so that the war might be fought more successfully.

31. Jerome Wiesner, cited in H. L. Nieburg, *In the Name of Science* (Chicago: Quadrangle, 1966). As Nieburg notes, "as the arms race has slackened [temporarily, as we now know], . . . space and science programs become a new instrument by which the government seeks to maintain a high level of economic activity."

32. B. Joseph Monsen, "The American Business View," *Daedalus*, Winter 1969. For important observations on these matters see Galbraith, *The New Industrial State*.

33. Quoted by John J. Powers Jr., president of Charles Pfizer and Co., in an address delivered to a conference of the Manufacturing Chemists Association, Inc. on November 21, 1967. Reprinted in the *Newsletter* of the North American Congress on Latin America (NACLA) 2, no. 7.

34. *New York Times*, May 6, 1967. Cited in a perceptive article by Paul Mattick, "The American Economy," *International Socialist Journal*, February 1968.

35. For some discussion, see Kidron, *Western Capitalism since the War*.

36. "A Brazilian View," in Raymond Vernon, ed., *How Latin America Views the American Investor* (New York: Praeger, 1966).

37. Nieburg, *In the Name of Science*. It might be more accurate to say that European capital finds its interest, in a narrow sense, best served by taking the role of junior partner in the American world system.

38. Quoted by Jacques Decornoy in *Le Monde hebdomadaire*, July 11–17, 1968. The series from which this is taken presents one of the very detailed eyewitness accounts of the Laotian guerrillas, the Pathet-Lao, and their attempts at "nation building" and development. Decornoy observes, in this connection, that "the Americans accuse the North Vietnamese of intervening militarily in the country. But it is they who speak of reducing Laos to zero, while the Pathet-Lao exalts the national culture and national independence."

39. Claude Julien, *L'Empire americain* (Paris: Grasset, 1968).

40. On this matter, see Andre Gunder Frank, *Capitalism and Underdevelopment in*

Latin America (New York: Monthly Review Press, 1967), and many other studies.

41. Bertil Svahnstrom, ed., *Documents of the World Conference on Vietnam* (Stockholm, July 1967).

42. *New York Times*, Bangkok, January 17, 1969. The writer is a bit naive in suggesting that the choice lies with the Thai. For some discussion of past "choices" for the Thai, see my *American Power and the New Mandarins*, chapter 1.

43. Cited by Hernando Abaya, *The Untold Philippine Story* (Quezon City: Malaya Books, 1967).

44. *Far East Economic Review*, reprinted in *Atlas*, February 1969.

45. *New York Times Economic Survey*, January 17, 1969.

46. Marcel Niedergang, in *Le Monde hebdomadaire*, December 12–18, 1968. Quotes are from the professors of the military college, who have constructed "a manichean vision of the world: the Communist East against the Christian West" in a manner that would delight John Foster Dulles, Dean Rusk, Melvin Laird, and other luminaries.

47. Cited by Akira Iriye, *Across the Pacific* (New York: Harcourt, Brace & World, 1967).

48. Nieburg, *In the Name of Science.*

49. Nieburg, *In the Name of Science.*

50. Speech at Millsaps College, Jackson, Mississippi, February 24, 1967. Others offer different justifications for managerial authority. For example, historian William Letwin explains that "no community can do without managers," those whose role is to make "arbitrary decisions within a private firm," for "the function of making ultimate arbitrary choices in production cannot be eliminated" ("The Past and Future of American Businessmen," *Daedalus*, Winter 1969). Letwin, who finds it "reassuring . . . that today's managers show the same vigorous appetite for income and wealth that spurred yesterday's businessmen to bold progress," fails to point out that on this theory of management, the manager can be replaced by a random number table.

51. "In the United States at the end of the fifties more than nine-tenths of final demand for aircraft and parts was on government, overwhelmingly military, account: as was nearly three-fifths of the demand for non-ferrous metals; over half the demand for chemicals and electronic goods; over one-third of the demand for communication equipment and scientific instruments: and so on down a list of eighteen major industries, one-tenth or more of whose final demand stemmed from government procurement." Kidron, *Western Capitalism since the War.* He also quotes an OECD report of 1963 noting that "the direct transfer to the civilian sector of products and techniques developed for military and space purposes is very small . . . [and] that the possibilities of such direct transfer will tend to diminish."

52. Kidron, *Western Capitalism since the War.*

53. Nieburg, *In the Name of Science.*

54. A major thesis of Galbraith's *New Industrial State.* A parallel analysis in the political realm is provided by Richard Barnet, with his investigation of the role of the National Security Bureaucracy in foreign policy. See his contribution to *No More Vietnams?* and his *Intervention and Revolution* (New York: New American Library, 1969). Without denying the relevance of his analysis, it is proper to add that the goals of this "organization" coincide with those of the great corporations, by and

large. Even in earlier stages of imperialism it was not unknown for the flag and gun to precede, rather than follow, the pound, the franc, or the dollar.

55. As Galbraith notes: "Goods are what the industrial system supplies." Thus "management of demand" performs this service; "it provides, in the aggregate, a relentless propaganda on behalf of goods in general" and thus helps "develop the kind of man the goals of the industrial system require—one that reliably spends his income and works reliably because he is always in need of more."

56. Lekachman, *Age of Keynes.*

57. "Like 1964's tax harvest, much of 1965's improvements would be realized by prosperous corporations and wealthy individuals" (Lekachman, *Age of Keynes*). The regressive character of the American tax structure is often overlooked. See Gabriel Kolko, *Wealth and Power in America: An Analysis of Social Class and Income Distribution* (New York: Praeger, 1962). The current report of the Council of Economic Advisers to Congress notes that: "As a share of income, higher taxes are paid by households in the lower income classes than by those with incomes between $6,000 and $15,000. This reflects the heavy tax burden on low-income families from State and local taxes. . . . Federal taxes also contribute to this burden through the social security payroll tax." The devices for tax avoidance in higher brackets have been discussed at length, the oil-depletion allowance being only the most notorious example.

58. For a reasoned analysis, see Michael Harrington, *Toward a Democratic Left* (New York: Macmillan, 1968). See also the review by Christopher Lasch in the *New York Review of Books*, July 11, 1968.

59. Harrington, *Toward a Democratic Left.*

60. See the contribution to Priscilla Long, ed., *The New Left* (Boston: Porter Sargent, 1970) by Paul Mattick. For an informative survey, strongly biased against radical hopes, see Adolf Sturmthal, *Workers' Councils: A Study of Workplace Organization on Both Sides of the Iron Curtain* (Cambridge, MA: Harvard University Press, 1964).

61. See, for example, Adam Ulam, *The Unfinished Revolution* (New York: Random House, 1960). He suggests that "a vigorous growth of capitalism helps the growth of Marxist socialism among the workers; but, also, a speedy extinction by Marxism of syndicalist and anarchistic feelings among the workers can be a contributing factor to the flourishing development of capitalism! The lesson of Marxism has been absorbed by the worker: he works more efficiently since he accepts the inevitability of industrial labor and its appurtenances; his class hostility does not find expression in sabotage of the industrial and political system that he expects to inherit." In short, the revolutionary movement can contribute, in striking opposition to its goals, to the creation of a "race of patient and disciplined workers" (Ulam, quoting Arthur Redford).

62. Parts of this statement are reprinted in Mitchell Cohen and Dennis Hale, ed., *The New Student Left: An Anthology*, 2nd ed. (Boston: Beacon Press, 1967).

63. *New Left Notes*, December 11, 1968. It is difficult for me to believe that the author, who knows Harvard well, really thinks of Nathan Pusey as the representative of imperialism on the Harvard campus.

64. Recall George Orwell's painfully accurate characterization: "Particularly on the

Left, political thought is a sort of masturbation fantasy in which the world of fact hardly matters."

TWO: AN EXCEPTION TO THE RULES

1. William Quandt, *Decade of Decisions: American Policy Toward the Arab-Israeli Conflict, 1967-1976* (Berkeley: University of California Press, 1977).
2. Charles W. Yost, "The Arab-Israeli War," *Foreign Affairs*, January 1968; Yost takes this to have been "the curtain-raiser to the Six Day War."
3. John Cooley, *Green March, Black September: The Story of the Palestinian Arabs* (London: Frank Cass Publishers, 1973).
4. Yahuda Slutzky, *Sefer Toldot Hahaganah* [*The History of the Haganah*] (Tel Aviv: Zionist Library, 1972).

THREE: THE DIVINE LICENSE TO KILL

1. Richard Wightman Fox, *Reinhold Niebuhr: A Biography* (New York: Pantheon, 1985); Robert McAfee Brown, ed., *The Essential Reinhold Niebuhr: Selected Essays and Addresses* (New Haven, CT: Yale University Press, 1986). Quotes drawn from these; or, unless otherwise indicated, reviews or jacket cover comments for these books: David Brion Davis, *New York Review of Books*, February 13, 1986; Christopher Lasch, *In These Times*, March 26, 1986; Paul Roazen, *New Republic*, March 31, 1986. Bundy cited by Davis. Schlesinger, also "Reinhold Niebuhr's Role in Political Thought," in Charles W. Kegley and Robert W. Bretall, eds., *Reinhold Niebuhr: His Religious, Social, and Political Thought* (New York: Macmillan, 1956). Kenneth W. Thompson, *Words and Deeds in Foreign Policy*, Fifth Annual Morgenthau Memorial Lecture (New York: Council on Religion and International Affairs, 1986).
2. Further references below given in the body of the chapter are, unless otherwise noted, to the two volumes of this work.
3. Reinhold Niebuhr, "The Christian Church in a Secular Age," 1937, in Brown, ed., *The Essential Reinhold Niebuhr*; my emphasis.
4. Reinhold Niebuhr, "Optimism, Pessimism, and Religious Faith," 1940, in Brown, ed., *The Essential Reinhold Niebuhr*.
5. Sidney Hook, *Towards the Understanding of Karl Marx* (New York: John Day, 1933).
6. Reinhold Niebuhr, *The Irony of American History* (New York: Charles Scribner's Sons, 1952), p. 115.
7. See Nathan Miller, *The Founding Finaglers* (New York: David McKay, 1976).
8. Hans J. Morgenthau, *In Defense of the National Interest: A Critical Examination of American Foreign Policy* (New York: Alfred A. Knopf, 1951).

FOUR: "CONSENT WITHOUT CONSENT": REFLECTIONS ON THE THEORY AND PRACTICE OF DEMOCRACY

1. This chapter is reprinted by permission of *Cleveland State Law Review*.
2. Jeffrey H. Birnbaum, "As Clinton Is Derided as Flaming Liberal by GOP, His Achievements Look Centrist and Pro-Business," *Wall Street Journal*, October 7,

1994, p. A12; Rick Wartzman, "Special Interests, With Backing of GOP, Defeat Numerous White House Efforts," *Wall Street Journal,* October 7, 1994, p. A12; and David Broder and Michael Weiskopf, "Finding New Friends on the Hill," *Washington Post National Weekly,* October 3–9, 1994.

3.   Susan B. Garland and Mary Beth Regan, with Paul Magnusson and John Carey, "Back to the Trenches," *Business Week,* September 17, 1995, p. 42.

4.   Helene Cooper, "Ron Brown Worked Tirelessly for U.S. Industry But Got Little Support from Business in Return," *Wall Street Journal,* April 5, 1996, p. A10.

5.   Thomas Ferguson, *Golden Rule: The Investment Theory of Party Competition and the Logic of Money-Driven Political Systems* (Chicago: University of Chicago Press, 1995).

6.   Everett Carl Ladd, "The 1994 Congressional Elections: The Postindustrial Realignment Continues," *Political Sociology* 110 (Spring 1995); John Dillin, "Brown Refuses to Endorse Clinton," *Christian Science Monitor,* July 14,1992, p. 2; Greer, Margolis, Mitchell, Burns & Associates, *Being Heard: Strategic Communications Report and Recommendation,* prepared for AFL-CIO, March 21, 1994; and "America, Land of the Shaken," *Business Week,* March 11, 1996, p. 64.

7.   On the early postwar period, see Elizabeth Fones-Wolf, *Selling Free Enterprise: The Business Assault on Labor and Liberalism, 1945–60* (Urbana-Champaign, IL: University of Illinois Press, 1994). On the mid-1980s, see Vicente Navarro, "The 1984 Election and the New Deal," *Social Policy,* Spring 1985; Thomas Ferguson and Joel Rogers, "The Myth of America's Turn to the Right," *Atlantic,* May 1986; and Ferguson and Rogers, *Right Turn: The Decline of the Democrats and the Future of American Politics* (New York: Hill & Wang, 1986).

8.   *Los Angeles Times,* November 20, 1994, cited by Doug Henwood in "The Raw Deal," *Nation,* December 12,1994, p. 711.

9.   Mark N. Vamos, "Portrait of a Skeptical Public," *Business Week,* November 20, 1995, p. 138.

10.   Alex Carey, *Taking the Risk Out of Democracy: Propaganda in the US and Australia* (Sydney: University of New South Wales Press, 1995); Fones-Wolf, *Selling Free Enterprise,* p. 52 and 177.

11.   Jason DeParle, "Class is No Longer a Four-Letter Word," *New York Times Magazine,* March 17, 1996, p. 40.

12.   Kim Moody, *An Injury to All : The Decline of American Unionism* (New York: Verso, 1988), p. 147.

13.   Fones-Wolf, *Selling Free Enterprise,,* pp. 44–45 and 117.

14.   Meg Greenfield, "Back to Class War," *Newsweek,* February 12, 1996, p. 84; Editorial, "The Backlash Building against Business," *Business Week,* February 18, 1996, p. 102; John Liscio, "Is Inflation Tamed? Don't Believe It," *Barron's,* April 15, 1996, pp. 10–11.

15.   See Charles Sellers, *The Market Revolution: Jacksonian America, 1815–1846* (Oxford: Oxford University Press, 1991), p. 106; Alexis De Tocqueville, *Democracy in America,* ed. Phillips Bradley (New York: Alfred A. Knopf, 1945), vol. 2, chapter 20, p. 161. On John Dewey, see particularly Robert Westbrook, *John Dewey and American Democracy* (Ithaca, NY: Cornell University Press, 1991).

16.   Norman Ware, *The Industrial Worker 1840–1860* (Chicago: Ivan R. Dee, 1990).

17. James Perry, "Notes From the Field," *Wall Street Journal*, February 26, 1996, p. A20.
18. Ferguson, *Golden Rule*, p. 72.
19. Albert R. Hunt, "Politics and People: The Republicans' Claiming High Ground," *Wall Street Journal*, February 22, 1996, p. A15.
20. Henry Adams, *History of the United States of America during the Administrations of Thomas Jefferson* (New York: Literary Classics of the United States, Inc., 1986), p. 61.
21. "Clinton Warns of Medicaid Plan," *Boston Globe*, October 1, 1995, p. 12.
22. Alan Murray, "The Outlook: Deficit Politics; Is the Era Over?" *Wall Street Journal*, March 4, 1996, p. A1.
23. New York Times/CBS News Poll, *New York Times*, October 1, 1995, p. 4.
24. Business Week/Harris Executive Poll, *Business Week*, June 5, 1995, p. 34.
25. Robert Siegel, National Public Radio, *All Things Considered*, May 12, 1995.
26. Knight-Ridder, "GOP Pollster Never Measured Popularity of 'Contract,' Only Slogans," *Chicago Tribune*, November 12, 1995, p. 11; Michael Weisskopf and David Maraniss, "Gingrich's War of Words," *Washington Post* (national weekly edition), November 6–12, 1995, p. 6.
27. Michael Dawson, *The Consumer Trap: Big Business Marketing and the Frustration of Personal Life in the United States since 1945*, Ph.D. Dissertation, University of Oregon, August 1995.
28. Edward L. Bernays, *Propaganda* [1928] (Brooklyn: Ig Publishing, 2004).
29. David S. Fogelsong, *America's Secret War Against Bolshevism: U.S. Intervention in the Russian Civil War, 1917–1920* (Chapel Hill, NC: University of North Carolina Press, 1995), p. 28.
30. Patricia Cayo Sexton, *The War on Labor and the Left* (Boulder, CO: Westview Press, 1991), p. 112; David Montgomery, *The Fall of the House of Labor: The Workplace, the State, and American Labor Activism, 1865–1925* (Cambridge: Cambridge University Press, 1987), p. 7.
31. Samuel Huntington, "Vietnam Reappraised," *International Security* 6, no. 1 (Summer 1981), p. 14.
32. See Frank Kofksy, *Harry S. Truman and the War Scare of 1948* (New York: Macmillan, 1993); Noam Chomsky, *Turning the Tide: U.S. Intervention in Central America and the Struggle for Peace*, expanded ed. (Boston: South End Press, 1985), a new edition of which is forthcoming in 2015 from Haymarket Books; Noam Chomsky, *World Orders, Old and New,* expanded edition (New York: Columbia University Press, 1996).
33. Eyal Press, "GOP 'Responsibility' on US Arms Sales," *Christian Science Monitor*, February 23, 1995, p. 19.
34. Gerald K. Haines, *The Americanization of Brazil: A Study of U.S. Cold War Diplomacy in the Third World, 1945–1954* (Wilmington, DE: Scholarly Resources, 1989), pp. ix, 121.
35. Stephen Streeter, "Campaigning against Latin American Nationalism: John Moors Cabot in Brazil, 1959–1961," *The Americas* 51, no. 2 (October 1994), pp. 193–218, citing a report to the National Security Council, May 21, 1958.
36. John Foster Dulles, Telephone Call to Allen Dulles, "Minutes of telephone conversations of John Foster Dulles and Christian Herter," June 19, 1958 (Eisenhower Presidential Library, Abilene, KS).

37. Thomas Carothers, "The Reagan Years: The 1980s," in Abraham Lowenthal, ed., *Exporting Democracy: The United States and Latin America* (Baltimore, MD: Johns Hopkins University Press, 1991), pp. 90–122; Thomas Carothers, *In the Name of Democracy: U.S. Policy Toward Latin America in the Reagan Years* (Berkeley, CA: University of California Press, 1991), p. 249.

38. Richard Bernstein, "The U.N. versus the U.S.," *New York Times Magazine*, January 22, 1984, p. 18.

39. Abram Sofaer, "The United States and the World Court," U.S. Department of State, Bureau of Public Affairs, *Current Policy*, no. 769 (December 1985), statement before the Senate Foreign Relations Committee. I am indebted to Tayyab Mahmud for bringing this to my attention.

40. Robert Fogelnest, "President's Column," *The Champion*, March 1996, p. 5.

41. Stuart Creighton Miller, *Benevolent Assimilation: The American Conquest of the Philippines, 1899–1903* (New Haven, CT: Yale University Press, 1982), pp. 74, 78, and 123.

42. *Allen v. Diebold, Inc.,* 33 F. 3d 674 (United States Court of Appeals, Sixth Circuit, decided September 6, 1994).

43. Francis Hutcheson, *A System of Moral Philosophy* [1755] (New York: August M. Kelley, 1968); Sheldon Gelman, "'Life' and 'Liberty': Their Original Meaning, Historical Antecedents, and Current Significance in the Debate over Abortion Rights," *Minnesota Law Review* 78, no. 585 (February 1994), p. 644, citing Hutcheson, *A System of Moral Philosophy*, p. 231.

44. See Gordon S. Wood, *The Radicalism of the American Revolution* (New York: Vintage, 1991), p. 245.

45. James G. Wilson, "The Role of Public Opinion in Constitutional Interpretation," *Brigham Young University Law Review* 1993, no. 4 (November 1993), p. 1055, quoting John Randolph, *Considerations on the Present State of Virginia* (1774).

46. Important recent studies include Jennifer Nedelsky, *Private Property and the Limits of American Constitutionalism: The Madisonian Framework and Its Legacy* (Chicago: University of Chicago Press, 1990); Richard Matthews, *If Men Were Angels: James Madison and the Heartless Empire of Reason* (Lawrence, KS: University Press of Kansas, 1994); Lance Banning, *The Sacred Fire of Liberty: James Madison and the Founding of the Federal Republic* (Ithaca, NY: Cornell University Press, 1995).

47. Jonathan Elliot, ed., *The Debates in the Several State Conventions: On the Adoption of the Federal Constitution, as Recommended by the General Convention at Philadelphia, in 1787,* 4 vols. (Philadelphia: J. B. Lippincott Company, 1907), p. 45.

48. See note 36 above.

49. Gordon S. Wood, *The Creation of the American Republic* (Chapel Hill, NC: University of North Carolina Press, 1969), pp. 513–14. Wood's thesis is that the enterprise failed and that the "democratic society" that emerged "was not the society the revolutionary leaders had wanted or expected," grounded in republican virtues and enlightenment (note 44, p. 365). Whether the failure of republicanism led to a triumph of democracy, however, depends very much on how we understand the latter concept, and the events that followed. Many, including even much of the white working class, had a different picture.

50. Gerald Colby and Charlotte Dennett, *Thy Will Be Done: The Conquest of the Amazon; Nelson Rockefeller and Evangelism in the Age of Oil* (New York: Harper Collins, 1995), p. 15.

51. Sidney Plotkin and William E. Scheurman, *Private Interests Public Spending: Balanced-Budget Conservatism and the Fiscal Crisis* (Boston: South End Press, 1994), p. 223.

52. Vincent Cable, "The Diminished Nation-State: A Study in the Loss of Economic Power," *Daedalus* 124, no. 2 (Spring 1995), citing the *UN World Investment Report* (1993).

53. Robert Hayes, "U.S. Competitiveness: 'Resurgence' versus Reality," *Challenge* 39, no. 2 (March/April 1996), pp. 36–44. On the "bloated, top-heavy managerial and supervisory bureaucracies" of US corporations (more than three times as high as Germany and Japan), and the relation of "corporate bloat" to the (also unusual) US "wage squeeze," see David M. Gordon, *Fat and Mean: The Corporate Squeeze of Working Americans and the Myth of Managerial "Downsizing"* (New York: Free Press, 1996).

54. Judith H. Dobrzynski, "Getting What They Deserve? No Profit Is No Problem for High-Paid Executives," *New York Times*, February 22, 1996. For extensive data, see Lawrence R. Mishel and Jared Berenstein, *The State of Working America: 1994–95* (Armonk, NY: M. E. Sharpe, 1994).

55. US Department of Commerce, *Survey of Current Business*, 75, no. 8 (August 1995), pp. 97 and 112.

56. Bernard Wysocki Jr., "Life and Death: Defense or Biotech? For Capital's Suburbs, Choices Were Fated," *Wall Street Journal*, December 12, 1995, pp. Al and A5.

57. Peter Applebome, "A Suburban Eden Where the Right Rules, with Conservatism Flowering among the Malls," *New York Times*, August 1, 1994.

58. Joseph S. Nye and William A. Owens, "America's Information Edge," *Foreign Affairs*, March/April 1966, p. 20.

59. Larry W. Schwartz, "Route 128 May Be the Road to a Free-Market Economy," *Boston Globe*, March 22, 1996, p. 23, adapted from his article "Venture Abroad: Developing Countries Need Venture Capital Strategies," *Foreign Affairs*, November/December 1994, pp. 15–18, adding Boston's Route 128.

60. John Cassidy, "Who Killed the Middle Class?," *New Yorker*, October 16, 1995, pp. 113–24

61. Winfried Ruigrok and Rob van Tulder, *The Logic of International Restructuring: The Management of Dependencies in Rival Industrial Complexes* (New York: Routledge, 1995), pp. 217 and 221–22.

FIVE: SIMPLE TRUTHS, HARD PROBLEMS: SOME THOUGHTS ON TERROR, JUSTICE, AND SELF-DEFENSE

1. For sources, see my *New Military Humanism: Lessons from Kosovo* (Monroe, ME: Common Courage Press, 1999); *A New Generation Draws the Line: Humanitarian Intervention and the "Responsibility to Protect" Today,* expanded ed. (Boulder, CO: Paradigm Publishers, 2012); and *Hegemony or Survival: America's Quest for Global*

Dominance, 2nd ed. (New York: Metropolitan/Owl, 2004). In this chapter, I will keep to citations not easy to locate in fairly standard work, or in recent books of mine, including these.

2. Elizabeth Becker, "Kissinger Tapes Describe Crises, War and Stark Photos of Abuse," *New York Times*, May 27, 2004.

3. Telford Taylor, *Nuremberg and Vietnam: An American Tragedy* (New York: Times Books, 1970).

4. Edward Alden, "Dismay at Attempt to Find Legal Justification for Torture," *Financial Times*, June 10, 2004.

5. Justice Richard Goldstone, "Kosovo: An Assessment in the Context of International Law," Nineteenth Annual Morgenthau Memorial Lecture, Carnegie Council on Ethics and International Affairs, May 12, 2000.

6. Michael Georgy, "Iraqis want Saddam's Old U.S. Friends on Trial," Reuters, January 20, 2004.

7. On this and other such operations, based in part on unpublished investigations of *Newsweek* Saigon bureau chief Kevin Buckley, see Chomsky and Herman, *The Washington Connection and Third World Fascism* (Montreal: Black Rose Books, 1979).

8. Arnon Regular, *Ha'aretz*, May 24, 2003, based on minutes of a meeting between Bush and his hand-picked Palestinian Prime Minister, Mahmoud Abbas, provided by Abbas. See also Howard Fineman, "Bush and God," *Newsweek*, March 10, 2003, with a cover story on the beliefs and direct line to God of the man with his finger on the button. Also the PBS documentary, "The Jesus Factor," *Frontline*, April 29, 2004, dir. Raney Aronson, on the "religious ideals" that Bush has brought to the White House, "relevant to the Bush messianic mission to graft democracy onto the rest of the world"; Sam Allis, "A Timely Look at How Faith Informs Bush Presidency," *Boston Globe*, February 29, 2004. White House aides report concern over Bush's "increasingly erratic behavior" as he "declares his decisions to be 'God's will'"; Doug Thompson, *Capitol Hill Blue*, June 4, 2004.

9. Gordon S. Wood, "'Freedom Just Around the Corner': Rogue Nation," *New York Times Book Review*, March 28, 2004; Thomas Bailey, *A Diplomatic History of the American People* (New York: Appleton-Century-Crofts, 1969).

10. Historians Thomas Pakenham and David Edwards, cited by Clifford Longley, "The Religious Roots of American Imperialism," *Global Dialogue* 5, nos. 1–2 (Winter/Spring 2003).

11. Cited by Pier Francesco Asso, "The 'Home Bias' Approach in the History of Economic Thought: Issues on Financial Globalization from Adam Smith to John Maynard Keynes," in Jochen Lorentzen and Marcello de Cecco, eds., *Markets and Authorities: Global Finance and Human Choice* (Cheltenham: Edward Elgar Publishing, 2002).

12. "Iraq: Another Intifada in the Making" and "The Mood on the Iraqi Streets: Bloodier and Sadder," *Economist*, April 15, 2004.

13. Walter Pincus, "Skepticism About U.S. Deep, Iraq Poll Shows: Motive for Invasion Is Focus of Doubts," *Washington Post*, November 12, 2003. Richard Burkholder, "Gallup Poll of Baghdad: Gauging U.S. Intent," October 28, 2003. Available online at www.gallup.com/poll/9595/gallup-poll-baghdad-gauging-us-intent.aspx.

14. Anton La Guardia, "Handover Still on Course as UN Waits for New Leader to Emerge," *Daily Telegraph*, May 18, 2004.

15. Carla Anne Robbins, "Negroponte Has Tricky Mission: Modern Proconsul," *Wall Street Journal*, April 27, 2004.

16. *Envío* (UCA, Jesuit University, Managua), November 2003.

17. Martha Crenshaw, "America at War," *Current History*, December 2001.

18. See, inter alia, my *Pirates and Emperors, Old and New: International Terrorism in the Real World*, updated ed. (Cambridge: South End Press, 2002). (A new edition of this work is forthcoming in 2014 from Haymarket Books.) For review of the first phase of the "war on terror," see Alexander George, ed., *Western State Terrorism* (Cambridge: Polity/Blackwell, 1991).

19. Stephen Zunes, "U.S. Policy towards Syria and the Triumph of Neoconservatism," *Middle East Policy* 11, no. 1 (Spring 2004).

20. The Independent International Commission on Kosovo, *The Kosovo Report: Conflict, International Response, Lessons Learned* (Oxford: Oxford University Press, 2000).

21. Goldstone, "Kosovo."

22. For review, see my *New Military Humanism*.

23. For details, see my *A New Generation Draws the Line*, which also reviews how NATO instantly overturned the Security Council resolution it had initiated. Goldstone, "Kosovo," recognizes that the resolution was a compromise, but does not go into the matter, which aroused no interest in the West.

24. The only detailed reviews I know of are in my books cited in the two preceding notes, with some additions from the later British parliamentary inquiry in my *Hegemony or Survival*.

25. Nicholas J. Wheeler, *Saving Strangers: Humanitarian Intervention and International Society* (Oxford: Oxford University Press, 2000).

26. Carsten Stahn, "Enforcement of the Collective Will after Iraq," *American Journal of International Law* 97, no. 4 (Symposium, "Future Implications of the Iraq Conflict") (October 2003), pp. 804–23. For more on these matters, including Michael Glennon's influential ideas and his rejection of other moral truisms, see my article and several others in *Review of International Studies* 29, no. 4 (October 2003), and my *Hegemony or Survival*.

27. See H. Bruce Franklin, *War Stars: The Super Weapon and the American Imagination* (Oxford: Oxford University Press, 1988).

CHAPTER SIX: HUMAN INTELLIGENCE AND THE ENVIRONMENT

1. Ernst Mayr, "Can SETI Succeed? Not Likely," *Bioastronomy News* 7, no. 3 (1995). Carl Sagan, "The Abundance of Life-Bearing Planets," *Bioastronomy News* 7, no. 4 (1995). See also Ernst Mayr, "Does It Pay to Acquire High Intelligence?" *Perspectives in Biology and Medicine*, no. 37 (Spring 1994).

2. United Nations Climate Change Conference, December 7–18, 2009, Copenhagen, Denmark.

3. George Monbiot, "If You Want to Know Who's to Blame for Copenhagen, Look to the US Senate," *Guardian,* December 21, 2009.

4. Edmund L. Andrews, "Greenspan Concedes Error on Regulation," *New York Times,* October 23, 2008, p. B1.

5. E. L. Doctorow, *Ragtime: A Novel* (New York: Random House, 1975).

6. See Richard B. Du Boff, *Accumulation and Power: An Economic History of the United States* (Armonk, NY: M. E. Sharpe, 1989).

7. "Exchange of Rail Know-How Between the United States and Spain," SpanishRailwayNews.com, December 7, 2011.

8. Leslie Kaufman, "Among Weathercasters, Doubt on Warming," *New York Times,* March 29, 2010, p. A1.

9. David Chandler, "Climate Change Odds Much Worse than Thought," *MIT News,* May 19, 2009. See also the reports of the Joint Program on the Science and Policy of Global Change, Massachusetts Institute of Technology (http://globalchange.mit.edu).

SEVEN: CAN CIVILIZATION SURVIVE REALLY EXISTING CAPITALISM?

1. See John Bellamy Foster and Robert W. McChesney, *The Endless Crisis: How Monopoly-Finance Capital Produces Stagnation and Upheaval from the U.S.A. to China* (New York: Monthly Review Press, 2012).

2. Editors, "Why Should Taxpayers Give Big Banks $83 Billion a Year?" Bloomberg View, February 20, 2013. Citing Kenichi Ueda and Beatrice Weder di Mauro, "Quantifying Structural Subsidy Values for Systemically Important Financial Institutions," IMF Working Paper, WP/12/128 (2012).

3. Martin Wolf, "Comment on Andrew G. Haldane, 'Control Rights (And Wrongs),'" Wincott Annual Memorial Lecture, October 24, 2011.

4. See, among other works, Gar Alperovitz, *America beyond Capitalism: Reclaiming Our Wealth, Our Liberty, and Our Democracy* (Hoboken, NJ: Wiley, 2004).

5. John Dewey, "Education vs. Trade-Training—Dr. Dewey's Reply," *New Republic* 3, no. 28 (1915), p. 42.

6. Quoted in Westbrook, *John Dewey and American Democracy*, p. 440.

7. Kelly Sims Gallagher, "Why and How Governments Support Renewable Energy," *Daedalus* 142, no. 1 (Winter 2013), pp. 59–77.

8. Jon A. Krosnick and Bo MacInnis, "Does the American Public Support Legislation to Reduce Greenhouse Gas Emissions?" *Daedalus* 142, no. 1 (Winter 2013), pp. 26–39.

9. Steve Horn, "Three States Pushing ALEC Bill to Require Teaching Climate Change Denial in Schools," DeSmogBlog, January 31, 2013.

10. Bill Dedman, "Leaked: A Plan to Teach Climate Change Skepticism in Schools," NBC News, February 15, 2012. Brendan DeMelle, "Heartland Institute Exposed: Internal Documents Unmask Heart of Climate Denial Machine," DeSmogBlog, February 14, 2012.

11. Suzanne Goldenberg, "Secret Funding Helped Build Vast Network of Climate Denial Thinktanks," *Guardian,* February 14, 2013.

12. Grace Wyler, "Bobby Jindal: The GOP 'Must Stop Being The Stupid Party,'" *Busi-*

ness Insider, January 25, 2013.

13. *Science*, January 18, 2013.

14. Richard A. Kerr, "Soot Is Warming the World Even More Than Thought," *Science*, January 25, 2013.

15. Dean Baker, *The Conservative Nanny State: How the Wealthy Use the Government to Stay Rich and Get Richer* (Washington, DC: Center for Economic and Policy Research, 2006).

Index

© DON USNER

About the Author

Noam Chomsky was born in Philadelphia, Pennsylvania, on December 7, 1928. He studied linguistics, mathematics, and philosophy at the University of Pennsylvania. In 1955, he received his Ph.D. from the University of Pennsylvania. Since receiving his Ph.D., Chomsky has taught at Massachusetts Institute of Technology, where he is Institute Professor (Emeritus) in the Department of Linguistics and Philosophy. His work is widely credited with having revolutionized the field of modern linguistics. Chomsky is the author of numerous best-selling political works that have been translated into scores of countries worldwide. His most recent books are the *New York Times* bestseller *Hegemony or Survival, Failed States, Imperial Ambitions, What We Say Goes, Interventions, Occupy,* and *Hopes and Prospects* (Haymarket Books). Haymarket Books is reissuing twelve of his classic works in new editions starting in 2014. His web site is www.chomsky.info.